TRAINS

To Nancy

Miriam Winter

11/11/06

TRAINS

A Memoir of a Hidden Childhood
during and after World War II

MIRIAM WINTER

Introduction by Sidney Bolkosky

Cover Art & Design Jurek Denis

KELTON PRESS
Jackson, Michigan

Inquiries should be addressed to
Kelton Press, P.O. Box 4236, Jackson, MI 49204.

Library of Congress Catalog Card Number: 97-74923.
Winter, Miriam
Trains: A Memoir of a Hidden Childhood
during and after World War II
ISBN 0-9660162-0-3

Printed in the United States of America

Third, Revised Edition

Cover Art and Design by Jurek Denis
Photograph by Monte Nagler

To Romek, Daniel, and David

Contents

Introduction

In her extraordinary memoir of her hidden child experience, Miriam Winter communicates the essence of what it meant to be a Jewish child during the Holocaust—not a singular essence, but multiple, confused, layered, and traumatic. Loss permeates each page. She was, she says, "lost in a dark forest of 'nonremembrance'," a term which adds a dreamlike quality to her memories and which will find its mirror in literal loss in dark forests, a ten-year-old girl alone, successfully fleeing for her life yet paradoxically engulfed in "the death of nonremembrance." Even after the war she remained "in hiding," partially dead. Her silence reflects that of many hidden children who persisted in hiding long after the war was over. Indeed, in some respects, she acknowledges that her life still seems shrouded by a veil of unknown or unacknowledged memory. "After the war ended," she writes, "my past was closed like an old valise." That valise, packed, opens here and each word seems crammed, too, like portmanteau words, full of multiple referents, thick with emotion and synchronous meaning.

Voices and images from her life before the war emerge from associations with contemporary scenes or objects, like trains. Historians have begun to examine in considerable detail the procedures followed by the railroad companies during the Holocaust. Poring over bills of lading, schedules, timetables, accounting ledgers, travel agency records, memoranda, and official correspondence, scholars have uncovered what many consider to be one of the essential elements of the destruction of European Jewry. Yet none of those studies manages to grasp the personal consequences which afflicted the victims of the Holocaust: packed "like sardines" into boxcars, not enough air or space, dying from the moment they entered, their lives were severed forever into before and after the trains. Survivors recall those cattle cars in a variety of styles, some hushed, some weeping, others angry, others re-experiencing the suffocation, the smells, noises, weeping, humiliation. In literal as well as symbolic ways, they were death trains.

Miriam Winter's trains shared the terror of those others, yet the irony which she eloquently communicates throughout her book perhaps begins here: her trains carried her to new life while killing the old one. She attributes her "rescue" to "pure random luck" that she was on one of those other trains. Trains, where the most crucial decisions of her young life were made for her, loom among her most vivid memories; she remembers them—but not her mother's face. Trying to recapture that image, lost along with the affection and warmth it embodied, has meant reacquiring her own identity as well. The book seems to awaken from those reflections, as if from its own sleep. She recalls her mother's voice, the feel of her hand on "Mirka's"—the diminutive for Miriam—head; her grandfather's "white hand against the windowpane" trying to symbolically wash before praying each morning in the Warsaw Ghetto; the star on her jacket in Lodz; the armband she was forced to wear in Warsaw, and then her flight with her parents and brother to Ozarow, followed by her separation from them when her parents sent her away with a stranger. As she left home, Miriam's father instructed her on how to make the sign of the cross, gave her a piece of paper with the Lord's Prayer written in block letters, and ordered her to memorize it before her journey was completed that day. From that point, she wandered various villages and farms, deposited by her mysterious savior with different Polish Catholic families who, despite their harsh treatment, saved her life. No one else in her family survived. The memoir flows from merged recollections of written notes and letters, a stream of consciousness of associations, memories, and multiple contexts as if she lived and lives a multiple life, the old beneath the new.

This powerfully and elegantly written book abounds with painful ironies: the trains which brought her life as death trains carried others; her religious father who instructed her on Christian practice; the constant motif of no tears—she did not cry, not then, not when beaten, not when lost, not when terrified, living daily, hourly, moment to moment in fear from the time she was eight years old, a child turned adult at age eight. It informs us of the utter arbitrariness of survival which could hinge upon a circumstance like hair color. Her hair, a curse, dark and curly, she continually juxtaposes to the hair of other young girls—then and now. Flaxen and straight hair means life, dark and curly hair means death. She describes an eleven-year-old student who came to interview her a few years ago whose "hair is blond as safety." It is security itself, this hair color of a child; she finds it, Miriam/Maria, who writes of the time when she was eleven: "Childhood? Even the word seems ironic." Vividly describing her surroundings, the people who wandered in and out of her life, she speaks of herself analogically: she is a broken string of beads (a persistent metaphor); her life was as "tattered as my rags were," "derailed like a crashing train." Everything depends on concealment, hiding, not speaking, eschewing and forgetting her Jewish past, locking it away in the valise; concealed feelings demanded hiding the truth and blocking out specific recollections, "like a ragged patch on my woolen skirt."

Beginning at age eight, she endured a life in hiding, tortured by such things as childhood fantasies which reflected real terror and real danger. Infested by lice, she watched as gadflies attacked her charge, a cow in the field, rendering her helpless, wild, and she dreams that night of being discovered and unable to scream, beset by deadly hordes of non-Jews, angry, like lice or like flies. Later she would be tormented by her recollections of childhood oaths determining that she would not cry and that "I shall never admit that I am Jewish." And she sees herself, after the war, as "suspended between facts, belonging nowhere, having nobody, frozen in limbo."

Introduction

Unlike nearly formulized survivor memoirs which speak of lost families and retained integrity, Miriam Winter's speaks of confusion and lost identity. If some survivors write of themselves as heroic, she writes of herself as hardened, living in constant fear, with death at her side, wanting only to be legitimized with a true baptism which a priest denied her. The baptism, too, becomes emblematic of her hidden status, her lies upon lies and the awful consequences of such a situation for a child. "Child Survivors" and hidden children, "the last survivors," bore a vast range of suffering, lost their childhoods to ubiquitous fear which persevered long after the end of the Holocaust and the war. Miriam kept her secret from "my friends, from my diary, from myself." No mention of her recurrent, suppressed memories of her parents, her grandfather, Yiddish (the language of secrets kept from her as a child), Jewish lullabies, or her name appeared in her life after the war, perhaps more oppressively denied than during it. Why, she keeps asking, did she not search for her family? Why keep the secret? Why not reclaim her name? Why, why, why?

In the end, for this painfully honest, thoughtful, and articulate woman, come the questions. Haunted by that past, again oppressed by her Christian rescuer and others under the Communist regime in Poland, Miriam Winter, aided at last by some loving kindness, began to reclaim her identity as a Jew and as a person in the 1960's. Having fashioned a productive life and new family, she continues to wrestle with the demons of a child trapped in the Holocaust. There remains the interminable, doggedly determined, but still-fruitless quest for her mother's face.

Sidney Bolkosky
Professor of History
University of Michigan-Dearborn

Acknowledgments

I owe so much to so many friends. My first debt of gratitude is to Mark Harris for his faith in this project. Without his support and generous help this book would not have been written. I am forever grateful to Faye Moskowitz for reading part of this memoir and for her invaluable criticism.

I owe my gratitude to all my readers for their helpful questions and comments. I am especially grateful to the readers of the early versions of *Trains*—Brian Bouldrey, Elliot Ginsburg, Martha Joyce, Bill Melms, Aliza Shevrin, Lisa Walker, and Jerry Weinberger, for their encouragement and help. And to the members of my writers' group—Donna Acton, Mary Batterson, Gary Cale, Mark Harris, Jean Lantis, Garry Righettini, Gail Schomer, Ann Smith, and Marti Wright—whose questions kept me on track.

I'd like to thank my diligent copy editor, Andrea Olson. My sincere thanks to Sidney Bolkosky, Henry Dasko, Ann Green, Hank Greenspan, Tadeusz and Tamara Jaworski, Jean Lantis, and Leon Wells, for their helpful criticism. And to Renata Avinoam, Estera Baker, Sharolyn Buxbaum, Sandra Calmas, Denni Glick, Erna Gorman, Laurie LaZebnik, Bianka Ramer, Ann Shore, Elaine Solomon, Val Mahoney, and countless others who helped.

I am deeply grateful to Jurek Denis, who designed the cover, and to Monte Nagler for his photograph of the author. I wish to thank Kurt Ashley, Gary Hall, Aurelie Seward, and the staff of the Computer Lab at Jackson Community College for their expertise and help.

MW

The Name

"How did your mother call you?" asked Romek.

"Marysia," I lied. My name in hiding was Marysia Kowalska, but my real name was Miriam Winter. Lies saved my life during the war, and I didn't stop lying when the war ended.

"So, how did your mother call you?" It was December of 1962, seventeen years after the war had ended. "How did your mother call you?"

Marysia.

"How did she call you when you were small?"

Marysia.

"When you cried, and she whispered to calm you down?"

Marysia.

"How did she call you when you were out in the yard?"

My mother called me Mirka. They all called me Mirka. Until the fall of 1941, I was a daughter, a granddaughter, a sister, a niece, and we lived like a tightly knotted string of beads: always together. Then, the string broke, and I wasn't call Mirka anymore.

TRAINS

In Poland, if you walk on a sandy beach after a storm, you may find a small bit of amber—fossil resin of the prehistoric trees that were buried in the ground for millions of years. Its colors could vary from light yellow, like nasturtium in a village garden, to golden brown—like honey poured over a piece of dark bread. Amber is soft to the touch: it feels warm even on a cold day. Worn over a winter dress, amber beads evoke summer fields full of grains. Like the fields in Stykow.

Pierced, strung together, small pieces of amber feel light around your neck. If you wear those beads you will touch them often, and they will awaken your senses. Each bead is full of life; you can feel the past embedded in the beads.

Sometimes, a relic remains inside a bit of amber: a bug's wing, a piece of leaf, a splinter of a twig. This small bit of life enclosed in the translucent matter may tell about life as it was before the ice rolled over the prehistoric forest.

For years my own feelings lay dormant like a fossil insect inside an amber bead. Now, fifty years after the war ended, I want to uncover my past and learn who I was. I want to know a girl called home by Mother. I close my eyes and wait. I see a girl with long black braids, wearing a navy-colored dress with a sailor's collar, a sailor's hat, and white knee-high socks. I see two black buttons holding the narrow straps of my black patent leather shoes. I can't recall my mother's face, but I hear a soft voice calling, "Mirka, Mirka . . ."

The Name

For years I didn't speak about the war. People were killed. Parents watched their children slain. I survived. What was there to tell? Only the dead can tell. But when my older son, Daniel, went to school, his teacher asked me to meet with the students to tell them about my life.

"Were you ever in a concentration camp?" asked a boy named Kevin.

"No," I said.

"Have you been very close to being killed?"

At once I said, "No," but later, at home, my memory returned . . . a memory of running scared. All of a sudden I recalled a woman screaming in a crowded church, "Father, she didn't receive absolution!" I recalled my escape to a forest and the fear of being found out.

"Why didn't your parents try to hide your brother?" Ashley asked. Her brother, Eric, is seven years old. As any older sister would, Ashley feels protective of Eric, as I felt when I played with Jozio. Jozio, my little brother, was only three years old when I left him in Ozarow.

"Jewish boys were marked," I told Ashley. "In Poland, only Jews were circumcised. Who would risk hiding a three-year-old boy? I don't even know how he died."

A boy in a green sweatshirt raised his hand. "Did you try to find your brother after the war?"

TRAINS

"I didn't search for my family until many years later."

"Why?"

"I was still hiding after the war, and I was all alone," I replied. He didn't ask any more, but for me the questions continued.

Why didn't I try to find my family after we parted in Ozarow in the fall of 1941? I left them in a heartbeat, and my heart didn't stop pounding. After the war ended my past was closed like an old valise. I didn't have to hide anymore, but I remained in hiding. I didn't admit that I was Jewish. I wore my mask well and smiled often. I spent many nights and days riding trains; my life was marked by packing and unpacking.

I have very little memory because I lost my family. Adults pass on a sense of continuity to a child. I had nothing to help me recall life as it once was. Not one photograph, not one tangible object... except for a photograph of my faked first communion. A photograph of an event that didn't happen.

In 1991 I learned how they were killed. Late that spring, I went to a gathering of children who had been hidden during the war. I placed my note on a bulletin board:

"Do you know what happened with the Jews from Ozarow?" I wrote in black felt marker on a white piece of paper.

Someone left a note: "Call Chaim," a phone number, 718, Brooklyn Area Code. When I called, Chaim told me that the Jews from Ozarow were taken to Treblinka.

"When?"

"October 15, 1942."

The Name

"Did you know Tobiasz Winter?"

He didn't know my family. We were transient there, last stop in flight from Lodz, to the Warsaw Ghetto, to Ozarow. Years later my belated quest laid open frames without faces. As if my family hadn't existed, files filled with names of victims revealed no trace of them. Even today I continue to pursue my quest: a single bead of a broken amber necklace, I am still searching for the other missing beads.

During that gathering we sat close to each other telling our stories. In a voice choked off by tears, one woman cried out: "Why didn't somebody look for us after the war?"

It wasn't easy to find us. After the war, I buried my past. I neither talked nor thought about it. Still hiding behind a Christian name, I didn't even admit that I was Jewish. And yet, I longed for burial places. I walked cemeteries as if I could find graves there of my dead.

At first, until 1969, when I found my birth certificate, I wasn't sure of anything, not even if I remembered their names correctly.

Now, I walk back into the forest to find my past, but what is left is an absence of memory. Sometimes I see my family for a passing moment. My father with my grandfather at a table in Ozarow. Their heads are covered, and I hear them singing. A song I hardly recognize: *Borhi . . . borhi . . .* loud unison singing. I see my grandfather in a black Hassidic hat; I hear forced joy in my father's voice, *Borhi . . . borhi . . .* a skullcap on his head.

Sometimes, I can even look into their eyes, but as soon as I try to catch them, as soon as I stop to jot down what I see, they flit back into the dark corners of nowhere, and my memory is blank again. I am lost in a dark forest of my "nonremembrance," and I feel like a knight-errant on a futile quest. The forest is full of mysteries that elude me. They are unwilling to surrender. Sometimes an image like a seed thrown into a barrel sprouts in the soil of my memory. I want it to take root. But it is winter still, and the garden is dormant; maybe the seed catalogs that are scattered across my desk will bring new plants to fill the slope.

In 1979, I found two of my cousins: Celina and Edek. My grandmother Szajna was related to their mother. I didn't find any other relatives, but in 1972, I found Cesia, the brave Jewish woman who saved my life. In the fall of 1941, she took me away from my parents. She had no place to hide me, so she left me with Maryla.

Fifty years have passed since a loving voice called me Mirka. I try to picture, to taste and touch, to hear and smell; I try to catch the image of myself in Ozarow, to recall how it felt to be called by my mother. I try to hear the sweet endearing names: *Mirka, Mirele, Mirunia, Mirusia, Mireczka, Mircia*; when the house is empty I say my name. I record myself saying "Mirka" and listen in the dark. I want to know how it felt to be called by my real name. To know a girl called home from a rain in spring. Called home from a walk in summer. Called home, for the last time, in the fall of 1941.

Before

There isn't much I remember from the time before the war. I left my family and came to live with strangers. No one survived to help me remember. I had an uncle, my mother's brother, whom I liked a lot. His name was Szmulek. Black haired, short, with burning eyes, he was a frequent visitor in our household. In Lubicz, in my grandparents' house, we played in the garden. In Lodz, where I lived with my parents, we played in the park. He laughed louder and more often than anybody I knew.

I think that my earliest memory is of summers with my grandparents in Lubicz. A small garden surrounded their white house. The bedroom where I slept was upstairs, above their clothing store on the first floor. I liked observing people coming to their store. I see myself playing with another girl, a neighbor's daughter. I don't recall anymore what her name was, but when I close my eyes, I can still touch her long, brown braids and hear her whispers.

TRAINS

With my eyes still closed I recall other images: a garden on a summer day in a small town in Poland. Two little girls sitting on a lawn, playing. We are in a store selling and buying produce: long twigs of grass neatly tied into bunches of chives. We pretend we are seller and buyer: bargaining, quoting the price, paying with money cut from brown packing paper. Old black buttons imitate coins.

Was that the earliest memory of a girl I once was, or did breaking a doll's head come even earlier? Why did I do it? I can still see myself as a small child sitting on a bed with a toy tool set. I remove a toy hammer from the cardboard box and begin pounding on the head of a large doll. The doll has the face of a baby girl, and it can open and close its eyes. It closes its eyes while in a supine position and opens them when raised. I think I want to know what is inside. The hammer is small, and it takes me a long time, but I succeed: I pound a large hole in my doll's head, right where the skull should be.

I peer inside. I see nothing. It seems totally empty. I expect to find sawdust or paper or cotton. But no . . . it is just hollow. I turn the doll upside down and shake it, but nothing comes out. The baby's head is empty. There are no dreams or memories or songs or games inside this little girl. I hug the baby and tell her not to worry because I will take care of her.

Before

_____

I can't recall how my people looked, but sometimes my senses respond to unexpected stimuli. One winter night I detected a whiff of *czulent*, a traditional Jewish casserole of potatoes and beef, baked overnight in a slow oven. The smell brought back a memory of a Saturday morning at a time when I was still with my family. Back then, if it smelled like *czulent* it was Saturday. Now, as an older woman, I am still striving to recall the image of a girl returning home on a cold wintry day to a world full of aromas.

I closed my eyes, trying to prolong the sensation in order to catch a glimpse of their faces—of one face at least. But I couldn't see my mother. The face seemed to be there for a passing moment, but it floated away. I did see her dress: a dark-violet, pleated georgette; but just a dress, without a person inside.

On another day, while driving alone, I heard a Yiddish lullaby played on the radio. Overcome with emotion, I began to cry in the car. I felt as though I was again in Ozarow. I could see the room. I centered my inner eye on that room so I could see my family, but what I saw were only faceless shapes. Walls without people. Afterward I sought out other recordings of Yiddish lullabies, hoping that the melody would again stir my memory and help me catch a glimpse of my mother's face. I think that I partially succeeded.

I loved my mother. She was slight, with dark chestnut hair pulled up around her face. Her name was Majta-Laja, but she was called Lonka. She had one fingernail growing irregularly on her right index finger, and I jokingly told her that she didn't need a thimble for her sewing. I recall sitting on her lap, being hugged, her soft hand touching my head.

I do remember Cesia, the woman who took me from my parents to safety. There was a boy sitting next to her when we drove away. His name was Stefan. In fact, I remembered Cesia's look so well that I recognized her immediately when, after finding her in 1972, I saw her in 1980.

For no apparent reason I also remember a face of an old woman who came to our crowded compartment during one long train ride. I even remember the year—1943, one year before the front line moved through the woods of Rzeszowszczyzna. What's in between is still a puzzle. The time between November, 1941 and spring 1942 is full of places; of long night train rides from one place to another. In my mind's eye I see countless train stops, towns' names printed in large block letters. "Tarnow, Rzeszow." I see the train stops of my lost childhood, and I hear these conductor's calls, but I always miss one track—the track back to my total past.

Questions help. "How did Maryla know when to move you to the next place?" asked my friend Mark. That made me see how often I had moved.

"How did you remember all the places?" asked a girl named Kelly.

I had them written down. At thirteen, in Zabkowice, I started a diary, and on the back page of the notebook I listed places from my childhood before hiding, when I was still with my parents:

Before

Lodz, Ozorkow, Torun, Rabka, Wisniowa Gora, Tuszyn Las, and Lodz again, this time amid the guns of war.

I remember moving from Lodz to Warsaw. I remember living with my family in the Warsaw Ghetto. The last place where we were together was Ozarow.

———— ⍟

When the war began I was six years old. I can still see this picture: We are walking home to Lodz from Tuszyn Las. The highway is packed with people, bundles on carts, baby carriages, bicycles, little carts, wheelbarrows full of clothing, bedding, toys. On the next picture is a rectangle crossed with white tape. A window is crossed with a sign of a letter **X**. Tape has been put over the window to protect the glass from the bombs. We are back in Lodz; Mother is putting paper tape over the window and I am eager to help her, but I can't reach to the top of the window.

————

On September 1, 1939, when the war began, I was still in Tuszyn Las, a small summer retreat close to Lodz. It was close enough to Lodz so that Father could come down every Friday afternoon and then return to his clothing store on Monday.

I played cops-and-robbers games with my friends. The oldest boy, a second grader, had a wristwatch and got to be the police chief in every game. We ran in the woods during long summer days.

In the next image we are also running, but the sound of laughter is sharply contrasted with the sound of gunshots, screams, and cries. Planes are flying low above our heads. I remember a long procession of people—women, children, old people—and of carts, bicycles, and wagons on a highway leading from Tuszyn Las to Lodz. I remember my little brother, Jozio, in his baby buggy. I remember a bundle tied to the handle of the baby cart and a long walk along the crowded highway with the German planes flying over our heads.

The next picture is of my maternal grandparents, the Kohns, arriving in Lodz wearing layers of clothing, dressed too warmly for the autumn day, carrying their belongings in bundles. They were forced to leave everything at once. They left their clothing store in the small town of Lubicz in the northern part of Poland, where they had lived all their lives. They were forced out of the home they had built when they were still very young. They left behind a tree they had planted when their daughter Lonka was born, and a garden where I made nosegays from forget-me-nots.

The next image is of the yellow star. An evening in our apartment in Lodz: Mother fastening the yellow star onto my dark-blue coat. We all sat around the table in the dining room, lamp lit, cutting out six-cornered stars from a piece of yellow cloth.

Jews were not allowed to be seen without the yellow star. From that evening on, whenever I went outside I had to wear my coat with the sign sewn on. I wore this sign on the front and the back of my coat until we got to Warsaw. There, in the Warsaw Ghetto, I wore a white armband with a blue Star of David.

Born on June 2, 1933, I was six years old in the fall of 1939, when we left Lodz for Warsaw. I remember a black car that took me from Lodz after the war began. Sitting in the backseat, on my grandmother's lap, I tried to understand why we had left home. I didn't know where we were going or why. I didn't get to pack my books. I knew that we wouldn't ever come back to my white bedroom with its creamy white furniture. Why did we leave my favorite dress hanging in the wardrobe? We stopped somewhere. A policeman told us to leave. We were searched. Then, we drove again.

It is September, 1993, and another girl has come to interview me for a class project. Her name is Catherine. She is fourteen, tall, strong, and mature. Notebook in her hand, she looks straight into my eyes and asks logical, pertinent questions.

In a book about the Warsaw Ghetto, Catherine saw pictures of starving children.

TRAINS

"Was it like that for you?" she asks.

"No, I am alive. I didn't starve. I got out of the Ghetto early."

What do I remember from the Warsaw Ghetto? I was with my family. They loved me. They tried to hide their fears. To make me feel secure, they talked to me. We lived in one room. They touched me and made me feel loved.

My maternal grandfather, Szymon Kohn, was a Hassid. He wore a black hat that accentuated the whiteness of his skin. When praying, he covered his shoulders with a large woolen prayer shawl, the *tallis*, and tied *tefillin* (phylacteries) to his arms and forehead. Chanting in Hebrew, he moved his thin body back and forth.

In the Warsaw Ghetto, during the very cold winter of 1940, when he was already too weak to leave his bed, he extended his fingers to the window to moisten them against the wet glass. As soon as his hand touched the glass he began his morning prayers. He wouldn't greet me in the morning before he said his prayers; he wouldn't pray until he washed his hands. This way, by touching the fogged window, he symbolically purified his hands. I still remember his white hand against the windowpane.

We had to wear white armbands with a blue Star of David. My mother stitched the sign on the piece of cloth with a blue thread.

Before

My parents made soap to sell on the street. The grayish looking soap cooked all day long on the stove, and the entire room smelled foul, like a dark basement. But my parents bartered the soap for food. We didn't starve.

Once my parents somehow got a large sack of potatoes. The potatoes were already frozen through. They were wrinkled and soft to the touch and, when cooked, had a peculiar sweet taste. Grandmother Szajna grated and fried them, which camouflaged their bad taste and odor.

After the freezing cold of the winter of 1940–41, still remembered in Europe as the coldest winter of the century, there came an unusually hot summer. The dust flew to my mouth when I walked the crowded street.

I don't know how my parents managed to get us all out of the Warsaw Ghetto. But they did. I remember a long ride at night, and I remember Ozarow, the place where we moved. We lived in a rented room in a small house on the outskirts of Ozarow. My father was ill. He had boils under his arms. My mother filled small bags with flaxseeds, boiled them for several hours, and then put them on his boils. The treatment didn't help, and my father was in pain for a long time. Nevertheless, I remember Ozarow as a clean, sweet-smelling place where I was happy with my family.

I remember dinners together, candles, Father and Grandfather singing. Coming home with Jozio one day I was reprimanded for not speaking Yiddish to my little brother. "Why do you speak Polish? Why don't you speak Yiddish?" asked an old woman sitting on a chair on the sidewalk. My parents talked Yiddish when they wanted to keep secrets from me and my brother. Even today when I hear Yiddish I feel danger, sadness, worry, anxiety, despair—all the secrets kept away from children.

In Ozarow, my parents continued bartering for food. Before the war they had a large clothing store in Lodz. They took along whatever they could carry: Mother's jewels, her diamond ring, some gold coins, large pieces of heavy wool for men's suits. Now they were exchanging for food whatever they had. Every day they went to the marketplace. They came back overjoyed when their goods were worth a grain of food. On one occasion a Polish peasant woman complimented Mother's brown purse, which she quickly swapped for a loaf of bread.

But often they returned tense and empty-handed. Sometimes I caught a fraction of their conversation, but they didn't discuss anything important in Polish. They tried to be discreet, whispering in Yiddish or sending me outside to play with Jozio. Yiddish gave them a natural disguise. They kept their worries away from the children, so that my memory is permeated by warmth, playfulness, even laughter. My memories from Ozarow came to life in 1979, when I found my cousin Celina.

"I was in the Lodz Ghetto with your uncle Szmulek," she said. "Your parents wrote to Szmulek from Ozarow. Those were good letters, full of hope."

The Trains

My recollection of trains begins with a still photo from a film, *Pociag* (Night train), in which I acted in 1957, while I was a student in the Theater and Film School, in Lodz. "Wear your red dress," suggested my friend who gave me the part. The film was black and white, but he wanted me to look good.

A man runs through a train trying to escape. The passengers notice him momentarily but return to what they are doing. I sit in a dark compartment, entangled in a kiss, concealed by a hanging coat. Those pursuing the escapee open the door, move the coat aside, uncover the kissing couple, and leave.

Gradually, I recall other trains. A train ride at night from Warsaw to Krakow . . . frank talk with a stranger the whole night long. It is harder to bring back the train rides with Maryla during the war. At first they are only dimly lit memories of crowds of people pushing, seeking space in dark, already-filled compartments.

I was on a train to Rabka when I first heard about the war. *Wojna* was the word I heard; I was on a train, and people were talking about the war

TRAINS

(*wojna*). I was four years old, and this was the first train ride that I remember. I was still weak after a bad case of measles. A doctor advised a short stay in a sanatorium. Rabka, in the mountains of Tatra, was the one he suggested, so Mother and I boarded the train and went to Rabka. Helping Mother pack my suitcase, I felt insecure. I heard adults whisper, and I felt their silence. The word *Germany* had a dark, foreboding sound. We went to Rabka anyway, as planned. Just Mother and me.

I remember letters from my father that were sent to me from Lodz. He printed large block letters on small pieces of paper. My letters to Father from Rabka were also printed in large letters on small pieces of paper. I tore a page from a notebook and wrote *"KOCHANY TATUSIU"* (Dear Daddy) in large block letters. I loved my father. He was short, bald, funny, and fast as a bullet.

When he wrote back, it was again in pencil, in large print on small pieces of paper. In my memory, images of those letters, large print in pencil on small pieces of paper, merge with another piece of paper with block letters that he handed to me on our ˙final good-bye four years later. I remember those letters from before the war, for there were no other letters from any member of my family. Never.

In Rabka I missed seeing Father, who remained in Lodz to take care of his store. I missed our nightly readings. "Slon Trabalski" (Trunky, the elephant), by Julian Tuwim, was my favorite poem. Each time that Father would read about this elephant who kept forgetting that his name was

The Trains

Tomasz, I would say in jest, "His name was Tobiasz," and I would look for approval into my father's eyes. His name was Tobiasz Winter, and he never failed to acknowledge my childish wit. And that's why I was almost sure I knew my father's name when the war ended.

Father taught me how to recite another poem by Tuwim—"Locomotive," in which Tuwim used Polish onomatopoeic words like *buch, uch, puff, uff* and rhythmic repetitions to express the sounds of a steam engine. These were words easy for a child to say, words expressing movements of a train from the first hiss of the steam engine to the full speed of a train in motion. I remember reciting "Locomotive" in a clandestine classroom in the Warsaw Ghetto. My body and voice moved with the train.

> najpierw powoli
> jak zolw ociezale
> ruszyla maszyna
> po szynach ospale.

Arms forward and back like the piston rods. Slow motion at first, then speed up the pace. Legs stepping into the gradually increasing rhythm of train wheels on the track: to tak-toto, tak-toto, tak-toto-tak . . . Gear up, step on it, hasten, hurry, rush, under full steam, rapid, speedy, double-quick, flee at full speed, like the wind, race, tear, dash, flee.

TRANS

przez gory, przez tunel,
przez pola, przez las,

The Polish word for forest is *las,* and I hid in a forest after my life derailed like a crashing train. I came to my first hiding place on a train. Other trains rolled their wheels, and I survived by a roll of dice, pure random luck. A life saved by chance, punctuated by train stops, hitting the metal tracks rhythmically: caboose, choo-choo, chums . . . tatata, tatata, tatata . . .

My life was saved through a chance meeting of two strangers on a train. One steam engine stopped at a platform in Kielce, where Maryla boarded a train and met Cesia. If Maryla had gone to another compartment I would have been killed. I survived, but I can't recall my mother's face, although I do remember the train that took me away.

———

"When the war ends, read newspapers," said Father. "We have family abroad; maybe somebody will be looking for you." He did not say, "I will look for you after the war." He did not have such hope.

Until that evening in Ozarow, my parents were looking for ways to escape. They were young and resourceful. They left Lodz on time; they even left the Warsaw Ghetto before it was completely sealed off. They still had some money, some jewelry hidden, and some large pieces of good English wool from their store in Lodz. But in the fall of 1941 the slaughter of Jews in Poland was put into motion in a well-organized way. There was no place to hide, no way to escape. My parents lost hope.

One evening in November a woman came to visit, and Mother sent me outside. I didn't know that it was Cesia. She was blonde, and she looked like a Polish woman. I didn't know that she was Jewish. I don't remember hearing Cesia's name at the time of our parting.

I remember my father teaching me how to make the sign of the cross. He sat me across from himself at the kitchen table. He gave me a piece of paper on which the Lord's Prayer was written in pencil in large block letters. He told me that from now on my name was Marysia Kowalska. He ordered me to call every woman I would be with *mama* and every man *tata* and never to admit that I was Jewish or that my name was Miriam Winter. He pointed to the lining of my dark-blue winter coat, where a gold coin was sewn for a last resort. That was all.

Riding away from my family in a horse-drawn buggy with a tall, blond woman I didn't know and with a boy of fourteen named Stefan, I wasn't crying. I sat deep in my seat reading by the moonlight. On a small piece of paper were words penciled in large block letters. I was memorizing the *Our Father.* My father, Tobiasz Winter, a religious Jew, gave me this Christian prayer to memorize as quickly as I could and to repeat in front of anyone who might look at me.

TRAINS

Our parting seemed uneventful. All I can recall are rushed actions, short instructions. No hugs, no crying, no kissing? What did I say to my little brother, Jozio? Where did Grandmother Szajna stand at the time of my departure? Where was Grandfather Szymon? Where was Mother? What did she say? How did she look? Did she touch me? Nothing. Only Cesia in front with the driver, Stefan with me on the backseat.

From that ride away I remember nothing more except a red scarf tied around my neck. There were no cries to break the silence of the ride. I kept my prayer note, repeating it again and again, quickly becoming an obedient girl who would memorize her new prayer and forget the face of her mother.

Years later, in 1980, Cesia told me how my mother begged her to take me away. Until then, I didn't know. I was eight years old. I didn't know that we were parting; I didn't realize that it was forever; I didn't know what I left and why.

Cesia, blonde, tall, and handsome, lived in Warsaw on the Aryan side. She supported herself by food barter, spending her days and nights on long train rides. Before the war she lived in Lubicz, where her parents were friends with my grandparents, the Kohns. When she arrived in Ozarow in the fall of 1941, she had a hiding place ready for her nephew Stefan. Taking me along was not planned. But my mother learned about Cesia's arrival in Ozarow, and she begged Cesia to take me away.

"I am twenty years old; who would believe me that I have an eight-year-old daughter?" Cesia said to my mother, but my mother pleaded and cried.

"What if something happens to her?" asked Cesia.

"Just take her," my mother said.

"How can I?" asked Cesia. "I don't have a place to hide her."

"Save my child!" my mother cried.

So, this brave, young Jewish woman took me on the spur of the moment. I didn't know that until 1980. Cesia told me about our train ride and about meeting Maryla.

———

When the train arrived we worked our way through the crowd and boarded. Cesia pushed us into the crowded compartment. She put Stefan close to me on the floor. We quickly fell asleep. Cesia covered us with a blanket.

She didn't know what to do with me. My curly, black hair marked me as Jewish. She couldn't keep me, and she didn't have a hiding place for me. She had one for Stefan, who at fourteen was already tall and strong. Blond like Cesia, he didn't look like a Jew. He would be a farm boy. We were already in the compartment when a woman entered carrying parcels of food. We later learned that her name was Maryla. Cesia made room for her. Maryla put her brown suitcase on the shelf above and smoothed her skirt before sitting down on the wooden bench. The train whistled and moved.

In the dim light of the lamp Maryla surveyed the train compartment and noticed us under the blanket. Stefan was blond like Cesia; my face and hair were covered by the blanket. The women began to talk. For a while, Maryla watched the slow rhythmic rising and falling of the blanket. Then, I turned in my sleep, releasing one black braid from its cover. Cesia moved from her seat, bent over the floor, and readjusted the blanket.

"Are those children yours?"

"Oh, no, they are my sister's. Poor Regina, she is always in trouble. She was left alone with two children when her husband died." Cesia quickly invented a story about her sister's second marriage and about her new husband's aversion for the kids. I moved again, and Maryla looked at my hair. "They were happy for a while, then a fresh trouble started." With her eyes fixed on the black braid Maryla listened to the story of Regina's husband.

"He is good to her but doesn't like her kids. He took an instant dislike to them, and things worsened quickly. So, to save my sister's marriage I offered to take them along."

Maryla looked at the blanket. "I would take the girl," she told Cesia.

Cesia shrewdly hid her relief. She didn't tell Maryla that I was Jewish. She wrote down Maryla's address in Lwow—Academicki Square number one. They both agreed that Cesia would take me to Maryla's apartment in Lwow. She gave Maryla some money received from my father and promised to give her more later.

The Trains

"Take good care of her," Cesia pleaded when they parted. I can only guess what motivated Maryla. Perhaps she wanted to have a child of her own. Perhaps she didn't know how hard it would be to keep me in Lwow. From Lwow Maryla took me to Czudec. I didn't see Cesia again until long after the war, in 1980. I know the train story from Cesia's recollections.

One year later, they met again on a train to Tarnow. And this time danger was very near indeed. Maryla sensed Cesia's panic when the news of a train raid passed through the crowded corridor like a telegram on a wire. Maryla reached for a bottle of vodka, took a large gulp and passed the bottle to Cesia.

"Don't let them know that you are afraid," she said and gave Cesia a slice of bread. When the train arrived at the station Cesia saw a German patrol standing on the platform. She wanted to get off, but it was too late. Maryla, who had covered this ground often on her smuggling trips, handed her another slice of bread, and a moment later Cesia saw the patrol boarding the train. It was crucial to be brave. Fear invited danger.

"Don't think about it," Maryla repeated, passing the bottle of vodka. Two drunken voices, one soprano, one alto, trolled merrily until the patrol passed their compartment. Afterward, Cesia gave Maryla some money.

"People in the village say that she is Jewish," said Maryla. "Is she Jewish?"

"Take good care of her," Cesia repeated, avoiding the question.

TRAINS

The food merchants moved in crowded trains. Each compartment was full of them. They always looked heavy at their waists, which were padded with slabs of meat. They carried bags and worn-down suitcases stuffed with bread, flour, grains, beans, whatever they could trade. Maryla was one of them. She moved food from the countryside to the city of Lwow. Later, she would move me from one hiding place to another. Maryla was tall and strong, a handsome peasant girl who had migrated to the city and made her own way.

The terminals were always crowded; the air was dark blue with cigarette smoke. On one occasion I was almost trampled; Maryla put me by the wall and, forming an arch, pushed the crowd away with the weight of her body.

Sometimes we traveled with Lilka. Lilka, the *Volksdeutschin*, was helping her friend, Maryla, to hide a Jewess. Maryla and Lilka worked in tandem, defying danger. Upswept hair, blonde on Lilka, dark on Maryla. Maryla had large round eyes, gray with a trace of green, fine cheekbones, a strong chin. Lilka's round lips with upturned corners made her appear ready to smile or to kiss. Her voice was soft like a whisper, but her small nose was as sharp as a hunting dog's.

On guard all the time, Maryla and Lilka could smell an informer from a distance, and keep him at arm's length.

The Trains

One day, when they were sitting on their suitcases
smoking, a man approached, bent down to light his
cigarette from Lilka's, and whispered something in
her ear. Lilka gave Maryla a sharp warning look
but continued flirting with the intruder until his
train arrived.

Without a word, Maryla took my hand and
walked slowly toward the train. A large valise in
Maryla's hand, her brown leather handbag in my
hand, we boarded the train going to Warsaw, not
our destination but away from the informer.

Fifty years later the sound of a pile driver reminded
me of trains. I was in Yad Vashem with other child
survivors attending the gathering of Hidden
Children. I learned that the Jews from Ozarow
were taken to the death camp in Treblinka. During
a memorial service, at the Hall of Remembrance,
my body pressed against the black wrought-iron
rail, I let my tears fall. Another survivor, a woman
named Elena, made me feel as I did in Mother's
arms when she gave me a silent hug. We stood
looking into the eternal light burning like a
crematorium. We looked down on a floor inscribed
with the names of the twenty-two largest Nazi
concentration and death camps. Treblinka was
below, on my right, nine block letters on a gray
mosaic floor.

TRAINS

From the Hall of Remembrance we went to the Valley of the Communities. Names of cities and towns, villages and shtetls were chiseled into the stone. I noticed Rzeszow high on the wall, Kolbuszowa, Ranizow, Radom, Szydlowiec, Kielce, Opatow, and then I found Ozarow—fourth from the bottom, on another wall. Ozarow was a temporary stay between the Warsaw Ghetto and my hiding places. Ozarow was the last place I was with my parents. I touched Ozarow; the sun-bathed stones returned my touch.

One man said, "I don't even know my name."

I told him, "If my brother had survived he wouldn't know his name either."

"Would you know how he looked?"

"No, I wouldn't."

This meeting with a man who doesn't know his name still lingers in my heart. Like me, he had many false names; like me, he survived alone. I am still searching, but there are no traces. I have often wondered why I survived. I am all that's left of the families of Winter and Kohn; if I hadn't lived, there wouldn't be a soul to say that they even existed. I am their witness.

Lwow, 1941

My hiding experience began in Lwow. I was eight years old when Cesia brought me to Lwow to live with Maryla in her nice, clean apartment. On the wall over a sleeper sofa hung a portrait of a young couple. Against the opposite wall stood a tall credenza filled with porcelain plates. In the center stood an oval table with chairs. Pots of pink cyclamens were scattered around the room. Maryla poured water into a white bowl underneath one plant.

"You should never pour water on cyclamen's roots," she said. From the large window dressed with lace curtains I looked down at the courtyard. Children's voices filled the air. I leaned down to see them playing.

"Don't come near the window. Don't let anybody see you here," said Maryla.

Cesia departed by train early the next morning, and Maryla went to work. For the first time in my life I was all alone. I missed being talked to and touched. Since the war started my grandparents, my parents, and Jozio, the six of us, lived in one room. I was eight years old. Until now my mother and grandmother, father and grandpa, and little Jozio were always around. They cuddled me and my brother, and they called me Mirka. When I closed my eyes, I could still feel someone's hand on the top of my head. I felt lonely and deserted. Cyclamens were blooming, but the apartment was cold, and everything was strange and foreign to me. The days went by. I did my chores. Daily I watered the plants, cleaned the apartment, peeled potatoes for dinner, and waited for Maryla's return. Polishing a large mirror in Maryla's bedroom, I looked at my reflection.

Even my looks had changed. When I came to live with Maryla I had two long braids of thick shiny hair. Parted in the middle, my black hair framed my small face, exposing blue eyes.

"What a pretty girl," said a passerby when I was sitting with my mother in a secluded hillside in Ozarow. Mother was brushing my hair. "She doesn't look like a Jewess at all," he said.

"Can't a Jewess be pretty, too?" asked my mother, still combative and proud.

A memory of this incident came back together with a feeling of my hair being caressed by a loving hand. At home mother braided my hair; I couldn't manage it all by myself. The braids were long, heavy, and curly. One day at the apartment, I tried to wash them, didn't rinse well enough, and broke a comb. The next day Maryla took a pair of scissors and cut my hair into a short bob.

And then I made my first mistake. The apartment was quiet, and I was supposed to keep still. One day, while Maryla was still at work, I was cleaning the kitchen when I heard laughter, then the barking of a dog, then laughter again. It seemed a long time since I had last heard children laugh. A narrow balcony surrounded the courtyard, and without a thought I sat at its rail peering down. A group of children played with a puppy. All the time I had been in Lwow I hadn't shown my face to the outside world; but, when I heard children's voices coming from the yard, I eagerly sat at the rail, fascinated by what I saw.

A sudden sense of immediate danger pulled me away. I stepped back into the apartment, but it was too late. The children had already noticed me and had begun to yell, (Zhidoova—Jewess) *"Zydowa! Zydowa! Zydowa!" Zydowa* is a hateful way of saying the word *Jewess*. I pulled the curtains together tightly, but the calls did not cease. Their screams kept coming at me louder and louder.

When Maryla returned the janitor told her what had happened. Early the next morning Maryla packed her brown valise and took me to the railroad station.

And so I came to Czudec. We arrived in Czudec at night in the deep dark of winter. The faint smell of burning wood blew up from the nearby houses as we walked along the dirt road from the train station to the home of a woman whom Maryla called Magda. The thatched house had an earthen floor. Magda lit a fire in a wood-burning oven to heat the room. She put bowls of soup on the table. The soup, made of sauerkraut and called *kapusniak*, had an odd taste.

Shredded cabbage, pickled in large wooden barrels, was a basic staple in the villages where I lived during the war. A pot of cooked sauerkraut was always on the stove, and later I got used to its taste. Sometimes it was cooked with dried beans. Often it was mixed with potatoes. Returning with a cow from the pasture I was happy to smell the strong aroma that signaled a hot meal. I enjoyed the satisfaction of quelled hunger after a long day in the field, but at the first contact *kapusniak* felt peculiar, like an unexpected touch from a wet dog on a chilly day.

Everything was unfamiliar to me here. I looked around the room while Maryla whispered to Magda. Until now I had lived in a city. The change from my previous life was so sudden, my memory didn't register many details, just the strange feeling of being an outcast. Maryla left me in Czudec, but I didn't stay long. I was called *Zydowa* again, so it was time to move. One day Maryla arrived by train and took me away. We boarded the train and went to Wola Rzedzinska.

And then it happened again, two years later, in another village one Sunday afternoon after church. Shading her eyes with her hand, Genia stood by a tree looking at me. Her black hair contrasted with the white dress that she had worn in the procession. I liked her. I liked watching the girls in white dresses throwing flowers in the church procession. Suddenly, she climbed the tree. Sitting on a branch of the old pear tree, Genia began to sing softly.

Enveloped in her soft voice I at first didn't realize that Genia was merely repeating one word— *Zydowa.*
"Why do you call me so? I am not."
"You must be; your hair is dark."
"Yours is dark, too."
"Yes, but I have straight hair, not curly like yours."
The song changed to incantation; Genia kept repeating *Zydowa* louder and louder. Exasperated, I ran to the woods. I stopped, found blueberries, drank water, but it didn't help. I could still hear Genia calling, *"Zydowa! Zydowa! Zydowa!"* The Polish language is difficult to translate because its many shadings are created by the degree to which the basic word is altered. *Zydowka, Zydowa, Zydowica, Zydoweczka, Zydzisko, Zyd, Zydek*, all these words derive from the same root—*Zyd* (Jew). "Words will never kill me," goes a nursery rhyme; except then—in German-occupied Poland, when Jews were singled out for killing—then, being called *Zydowa* possessed the power to kill.

The False Communion

Today is Monday, May 27, 1991. A gathering in New York City has brought together 1,600 men and women who, as children, spent the war in hiding or lived openly under false identities. During one workshop I hear a woman saying:

"Those hidden children who came from assimilated homes abandoned their Jewish religion in hiding."

I jump from my seat.

"My grandfather was a Hassid," I cry, interrupting her. Fifty chairs line the walls in a hotel room. We are sitting in a circle and take turns sharing our experiences. It isn't my turn to speak. "I wanted to be baptized; I have my First Communion Photo here with me!" I shout.

"So you were baptized."

"No, I wasn't. But I wanted to be."

All of a sudden I remember. Words, images, feelings, hidden, forgotten, never acknowledged, rush out, making me impassioned, disruptive, too loud, unruly, almost rude. I cannot stop, I tell them how quickly I changed in hiding, in Wola

Rzedzinska, when I was nine years old and alone with a cow.

Later, at night, I show the first communion photo to my Christian friend Teresa.

"Such sad eyes," she says, looking at the yellowed photograph of a small girl dressed in white with a white lily in her hand. "In my own first communion photo I was bursting with joy. Anyway, it is a memento of the way we were."

For me, this photo was much more than a memento. It defended me from Jew hunters. *She might be a Polish girl, although she looks Jewish,* they thought. At least they had doubts, or maybe they were afraid of God.

In truth, my First Communion was an unconsummated act. It never took place. Although the priest promised to baptize me and I underwent the required preparation, my First Communion didn't happen because the priest had religious scruples.

In November of 1941 Maryla brought me to stay with Maslowa in Wola Rzedzinska. Maslowa, a widow, lived with her three children in a house in the middle of the village. Jozek, the youngest, was still in school when we arrived. Her oldest son, Florek, tall, thin, with burning eyes and red cheeks, had tuberculosis. His sister, Helena, eyes as blue as her apron, greeted me and returned to her weaving. It was hard to see how Helena, with her blonde plaits wrapped around her face, could be Maslowa's daughter. Maslowa's eyes were small, narrow, hidden in a gray, wrinkled face. Her thin white hair was covered with a bleached linen kerchief. Her long, dark skirt, gathered at the waist, made her look short and sturdy. Next to Florek and Helena, Maslowa seemed even shorter than she really was. Helena's loom stood near the window. For a while I watched her weaving, fascinated by the journey of the spinning jenny as it traveled across the loom. The house faced a dirt road. "To go to church you turn right; to go to school, left," said Helena.

Later on, in Wola Rzedzinska, I went to the school run by the Catholic nuns. They were called *Siostry Sluzebniczki* "Sisters of Service." They wore black habits and white, starched bonnets, under black veils. One of them, Klara, had shining dark eyes and was often kind to me. The small child in a picture on the wall of the school made me think of my brother, Jozio, with his toes wiggling after a hot bath. "This is the Holy Family," said Sister Klara. Looking at that picture made me feel safe at a time when everything felt strange and frightening.

I was fearful of the farm animals. This started with a scary encounter with a gander shortly after I entered Maslowa's house. I had gone outside, pail in hand, to fetch water from the well. As soon as I appeared at the door the gander rushed after me. I stopped, and the gander curved his long neck and waited. Suddenly his neck uncoiled rapidly out of his soft white body. A strong pointed bill turned toward me from the bird's full height. When the gander stretched his neck his eyes looked straight into mine. He had met a weaker creature.

Now he knew my fear. He raised his head higher, and his beak came as high as my shoulder. Frightened, I ran inside. Afterward, each time I went outside, the gander charged after me with a flurry of white feathers and a loud shrilling sound; and every time I took flight.

On the morning after my first experience with the gander, Jozek, the younger son of Maslowa, tried to send me to the pasture with the cow. I tried to explain to him how frightened I was but he insisted.

"The cow is very large," I said. "I wouldn't know what to do with such a large animal."

"You will go right now," Maslowa said firmly. I refused again, and she hit me across my lower back. I turned, and she smacked me again. I don't recall crying. I felt shame for being beaten. I put a smile on my face and tried to ignore the pain. I forbade myself to cry. *I can take it*, I repeated to myself at night.

This first beating in my life was followed by others, and I hardened. But it was harder to live without tenderness. I came from a warm loving family. At home I was hugged, caressed, patted, kissed, and I missed it terribly. I longed for a simple pat. I wanted to be touched, but my life was devoid of any sign of affection.

My only attachment was to my new religion. I loved Jesus, I wanted to serve him, and I waited to be baptized.

My Jewish life was over for me. In the villages where I now lived everyone was Roman Catholic. I didn't hear Yiddish lullabies anymore. No one called me Mirka. When I was scared, or lonely, or sad, no one touched my forehead in a loving gesture.

With time my fear of the animals faded away. Day by day I took the cow to the field and stayed there until sunset. Now, the cow was my only companion, and farm animals dwelled in my imagination. At night, I invented peopleless stories. One story centered on a family of ducks: there was a father duck, his duck wife, and their seven children. I imagined them, prettily dressed, riding in a painted wagon to church on Sunday.

As time went by I adapted to the life in the village. I learned my chores and worked hard.

When was the last time I had felt Jewish? I remember. I was reading from a catechism, an old, worn-out book with folded corners and ripped pages. The cover must have been torn off. I don't recall a title page. Sister Klara had given me this book.

"This is a catechism; study it every day," she said.

I took my catechism to Maslowa's house and turned the pages. The room was dark and I sat by the fire looking at the pictures. One picture caught my eyes.

The drawing showed Jesus carrying the cross along a road lined with people. The cobblestone road (like the one leading to the church in Wola Rzedzinska) was lined with jeering, taunting, hateful people. Their faces were ugly and grimacing. The caption underneath the picture read: "and the Jews chanted: 'Crucify him, crucify him!'"

I came closer to the fire and read the caption again. I looked once more at the picture of the crowd. Each head was covered with a prayer shawl like my grandfather Szymon's. Each forehead wore a phylactery. Each face was distorted with hate. "Crucify him!"

TRAINS

I read by the glare of the oven, sure that I'd go to Hell. I was guilty because I was Jewish. I saw myself in the paws of the Devil. As I looked at his pitchfork I knew that he would punish me soon.

The Christian children from the village didn't have to hide. Despite the war they still lived with their families. I wanted to become Christian and also feel safe. I didn't want to be Jewish anymore. I memorized the prayers from the catechism. I had a good memory and learned fast.

The nuns lent me religious books full of tales of saints, virgins, and martyrs. One book, titled *The Lives of the Saints,* written by Piotr Skarga, had a story about a saint for every day in the calendar. Moved by their pride and defiance of danger, I wanted to be like them. I wanted to follow the martyrs, who chose to suffer pain rather than to renounce their religious principles. I decided to be a Christian martyr, like Saint Cecilia, who endured great suffering, fearlessly denouncing her oppressors, or a nun like Saint Theresa. When night came I drew the bench closer to the fire and read. I decided to become a nun. Other books had stories of good Christian girls, and I wanted to be as good as every one of them.

I was now a shepherd girl taking a cow into the pasture. Stick in hand I walked after the cow. Days went by in a monotonous progression. The early mornings when I took the cow out were the coldest and the last hours on the pasture the hungriest. When the cow was secured in the barn I would peel potatoes and start boiling supper.

Again, I try to see myself then. How did I look? I see a short, thin girl leading a cow by a rope;

walking barefoot along the path between the fields, covered with a dark blanket.

I had already outgrown nearly all the clothes I took with me when I left my parents. What did still fit was completely worn out. The navy, woolen dress that I wore on my departure from Ozarow had been remarkably long lasting. It came from a large piece of English wool that was purchased in the spring of 1939 and made into a suit for my mother. My own A-line dress came from a remnant of that piece and had a wide top and a trimmed sailor's collar. I wore this dress when I left home, but as I grew older the dress became too short. I cut the top off and wore the bottom as a skirt. My red dress had also become too short. Still it was a warm piece of wool, and I wore it as a blouse. As I grew it became smaller. Mended in several places it lasted me through the winter and then fell apart. When spring came I had nothing to put on as a top with my skirt except for a blue and white striped pajama top. Every Sunday I wore this outfit to church.

Waiting for the procession, the girls on the church lawn looked happy. Dressed in white, they sat calm, untroubled, safe, telling secrets. One, named Frania, was sitting in the center of the group, her white pleated skirt carefully arranged around her legs. "Pajamas," she said loudly when I was walking by. "Look at her, she is wearing pajamas to church."

––––––

My senses opened to smells and sounds that had nothing in common with the girl I once was. Life in the village centered on the church and revolved with the religious calendar. Seasons were marked by the labor in the fields. Late in the autumn women gathered in one house to tear feathers. The soft down was sold on the market in Tarnow. What was left was used to make a warm cover, a *pierzyna*, that melted the chills away on cold winter nights. We sat long evenings tearing goose feathers, heads covered with white kerchiefs, brows snowy white, noses tingling with flying down; even our voices seemed softer as we sang.

After Christmas we spun flax. We sat again on long wooden benches by the wall, singing and spinning linen thread. Carefully supported by the middle finger, the left thumb and index finger pulled on the grayish yellow fiber, twisting it gently. The right hand turned the spindle until it buzzed in the air, suspended on the even, smooth thread. Helena was one of the best spinners. Her spindle waltzed in the air like a dancer at a wedding.

My spindle didn't know how to dance. It hesitated and stopped often before turning; my thread was heavy, thick, ragged, and bumpy, unsuitable for weaving. During Lent we sang wailing lamentations on Christ's torment. One, "Ludu moj ludu, cozem ci uczynil?" (What have I done to you, my people?) pierced my heart like a thorn.

When I made flowers with Jadwiga and Teresa, Maslowa's two unmarried sisters who lived on the far end of the village, I learned more songs and prayers. They sold paper flowers on the open market in Tarnow. In winter I worked with them and learned to cut and curl pink tissue paper until it looked like a real rose. They sang religious songs while making flowers and taught me to sing with them. They showed me how to cut the petals from red crepe paper and form a poppy flower that looked real. They created roses from thin white tissue paper. Each cutout petal was bent with a sharp knife. The stems were formed from a thin wire and wrapped with a narrow strip of green paper ribbon. When each stem had two leaves attached, Jadwiga would gather them in a large wicker basket. Sometimes the sisters formed small bunches of flowers before they took their wares to Tarnow.

On winter nights they took me to vespers. The prayers intoned in the vestry wafted out into the churchyard. Long dark-yellow wax candles—*gromnice*—shimmered in the night. We walked back late, our steps sinking in soft-feeling snow.

Slowly the singing and the prayers carved a path into my heart. I went to mass every Sunday. I learned the prayers and said them often. In the back pew of the church I felt safe. Paper flowers on the altar: pink roses, red poppies, blue cornflowers.

The church smelled of warm wood and burned myrrh. My voice merged with other voices reciting the Latin prayers. In the unison of litany I felt at one with them all. My heart melted in the warm smell of wax candles and dissolved in the choral singing. When the sopranos soared I sat in silence, but the altos were soft, inviting, easy to follow, and I sang, merging my voice with the others, no longer estranged. My hand harbored dark rosary beads; soft to my touch, bending with my prayers. When at the end of the Holy Mass the priest intoned *Pax Vobiscum* in a strong dark baritone, I felt as if he proclaimed peace directly to me. *Et cum Spiritu Tuo* I sang back from the top of my lungs.

In the classroom I was praised for my quick memory. Sister Klara, the nun who was good to me, sometimes talked with me after class. One day before Easter Sister Klara asked the class why eggs should be blessed on the Holy Saturday. After a short silence my hand went up. "Because as a bird comes out from the shell so did Christ emerge from his tomb," I recited. Afterward, Sister Klara commended me warmly. She kept me in class when the other children ran home.

"The priest will baptize you soon. Then, you'll go to the First Communion with the rest of the children." My heart melted; I felt confirmed in my devotion, assured and accepted. From that afternoon on I studied the catechism even harder so I would be ready.

As soon as the snow melted, I took the cow to the pasture. I lived from day to day, waiting. I was lonely and cold, but my devotion grew along with my loneliness. Day by day I went out with the cow. The early hours were the coldest; the midday sun made me feel better. Going to church felt like taking a warm bath. All I wanted was to be baptized. I was waiting for a miracle, but the miracle wasn't going to happen.

Two weeks before the scheduled First Communion, the priest sent for me. I went to the church. Radiant pinkish yellow lit the far end of the sky, like a halo over a martyr's head. I walked toward the light. The sky darkened and it started to rain, but the light at the edge of the sky didn't diminish. The rain wet my face and I walked faster.

The False Communion

Inside, I put my right hand into the stone bowl filled with the holy water and crossed myself.

"Praised be Jesus Christ," I said, curtsying in front of the priest when I entered the sacristy. He extended his hand for me to kiss. It smelled of soft aromatic soap, like a pine tree on a sunny day. I was wet from the rain. My heart was pounding.

"I will not baptize you," he began looking at the ring on his finger, and I froze in place. "You may ask for it, later, after the war . . ." His words caught me unaware. He talked in a solemn voice, clearly articulating his words, but I couldn't understand them. I waited a long time.

"But, *prosze Ksiedza* . . ." I tried politely to argue, but he raised his hand and I stopped. His voice was cold. I looked at him with panic, but his eyes were still on the ring as he explained his plan.

"After the war, any priest will do it for you," he said slowly, as if he feared that I didn't understand. "I will not baptize you now when you may think that I am forcing my religion on you."

His mouth curled into a grimace as if he had bitten into a rotten part of an apple. "You have to wait for your baptism until after the war."

I sat motionless while he explained:

"You must pretend that you are making the confession."

My heart sank when I realized what he was saying. "I will be sitting there in the confessional, so it should be easy for you. But you must be very careful."

His large gray eyes were now looking straight into mine. I kept my arms folded, and the wet fabric felt cold against my skin.

TRAINS

"On Sunday you will not take the communion, but you must pretend that you are doing it. You must be very careful and do exactly as I say."

His words bit deep into my memory: "All you need to do is to imitate the motions of other children. You shall come to me for the confession, and I shall pretend to give you absolution. Then I shall pass you over at the communion. The sexton is prepared and will go along."

"May God reward you," I said, kissing his hand. I left the sacristy in a hurry. I didn't cry on my way back. No one ever talked with me about my condition, but I knew that crying would give me away. I squeezed my mouth into a smile and walked back to Maslowa's house. *I'll do what he told me to do,* I thought. I was barefoot and stepped from one cobblestone to another, which gave an impression of a carefree walk. Just as any nine-year-old girl would walk on a Sunday afternoon.

I heard a howl of someone's cow. I was close to Maslowa's house, and I slowed my steps and then sat at the doorstep. Seeing me there Maslowa said harshly: "Start churning the butter."

I poured cream into the butter churner and sat at the doorstep again. Inside I was crying. Moving my hands up and down I looked at the pear tree that grew taller in the passing daylight, and I repeated to myself what the priest had told me to do.

Saturday came, and I went to church to fake my confession. I walked slowly. I passed two boys throwing pebbles into a pond, then a group of girls laughing. "Tomorrow!" one screamed. Her voice cracked with laughter.

The False Communion

I turned my face away. I dreaded tomorrow. I had to pretend. I was afraid of what might happen in the church if anybody would notice. If I made a mistake. I knelt in front of the confessional among the village children awaiting their first confession. The priest went through the motions as if he was giving me absolution. But he didn't. I was excluded. I kissed his hand and moved away. In the dark corner of the church I bent my head and beat my breast, repeating *"Mea culpa, mea culpa, mea maxima culpa."* I felt rejected, deprived, and fearful. I was scared of what might happen to me on Sunday if I made a mistake. If I started to cry.

On Sunday I went to the church early. I needed time to prepare myself. When the village children gathered, I joined them, kneeling in front of the altar as if I was one of them. Together we moved to the pulpit. I moved a few steps closer when the next row moved. I did everything exactly the way the priest told me to do and waited fearfully for the divine manifestation.

I saw the priest coming. The sexton followed him with a small round silver tray. I opened my mouth and relaxed my tongue. No one heard the pounding of my heart. No one noticed that the priest had omitted one child. I pretended to swallow, bowed my head, walked back with my palms joined together, fingers unified in a praying gesture. I did not cry.

In a borrowed white dress I went with Maryla to Tarnow. I was short and thin. In a dress too long I appeared even smaller.

"What's your name?" asked the photographer.

I almost said, Mirka.

TRAINS

The photographer put a white silk lily into my hand and carefully arranged a picture of Saint Anthony on a small brown table.

"You are very quiet. Aren't you happy?"

He was loud and jolly.

"What name did you say?"

"Marysia."

"You have such dark hair. Marysia should be blonde."

He moved to his tripod, covered his camera with black velvet, and inserted a frame. It clicked like a false smile.

"My niece Dorotka also went to the First Communion today, but she doesn't look like you. That girl can laugh all day without stopping to take a breath. She's a riot."

He adjusted the lights.

"She has long blonde braids. Wouldn't you like to have long braids?"

His head was now covered. The black velvet muffled his voice.

"Now, smile for me, one, two, three, . . ."

The camera clicked; he removed the picture and the silk lily. The session was over. He folded the black velvet and put it on top of the table. Maryla paid, and we went back to Wola Rzedzinska.

The priest's refusal had serious consequences. It put me and those around me in danger. I had to pretend to be a Christian girl. Now it was harder for me to pretend. I was bound to make mistakes. I did. One day it escalated into a scream in a crowded church, and I almost lost my life.

The Confession

I walk through my garden in Jackson, Michigan, in March 1993. After the long Michigan winter, anxious to see new greens, I start tending my garden before all the snow melts. Every day I remove some of the frozen leaves covering the perennials. I push them away as soon as they thaw, carefully uncovering the new growth of red oriental poppies. I scatter lettuce seeds into a wooden whiskey barrel. Later, in summer, orange impatiens will sparkle in this shady area under a black walnut tree, but spring calls for the green leaves of lettuce.

A squirrel digs out an old walnut from the barrel: wet, dark, wrinkled, still hard as a stone. He sits on the edge of the barrel, holding the nut tight in his paws. *I will have to buy a new barrel,* I think. One hoop is rusting away, and the wooden staves are falling apart. I make a mental note to replace the old barrel, but my thoughts are now in Stykow half a century ago, closer to Gawel and his wooden barrels than to the lettuce and the squirrels of today.

TRAINS

Squirrels know how to puncture a shell and get to the core. It is harder to open the past than to crack a black walnut shell, but on this morning the rusted hoop, the old rotting staves, and the musty smell of wood all bring to me an image of Gawel making barrels in the thatched hut in Stykow. As if he were sitting right here, under my black walnut tree, I can see Gawel chiseling the wood.

I committed a grave mistake in Stykow in 1943. It happened in a crowded church during a Holy Mass. It happened by my own doing, and I stood there, fully visible, like a scarecrow in the newly plowed fields.

This year in Stykow was trying for me. I left Wola Rzedzinska shortly after the failed First Communion. Maryla had moved me to the Rzeszow region in the southeastern part of Poland. First, we stopped for a day in Hucisko, where Maryla's sister lived. Then we went to Stykow.

Maryla pretended to be my mother; I called her *Mamusia*. She had moved me to Stykow to stay with Gawel, his wife, Agata, and their daughter, Halinka. Halinka's brown eyes smiled at me. Two long plaits of flaxen hair swayed as she walked. We slept in the attic on a bundle of hay. Halinka taught me how to draw an image of a girl in a pleated skirt. On Sunday we walked to church together.

The Confession

When winter came we sang Christmas carols. Halinka liked to sing. She had a small voice pleasing in sound. Returning from the field in a gloomy mood I'd see Halinka in the middle of the room, arms akimbo, laughing. The Gawels lived in one room. Their hut was small, with a thatched roof and a clay floor. Cabbage stewed in the large kettle on the stove. In the summer, I took the cow to the pasture and worked in the fields. During the winter I took care of the cow, helped around the house, and watched Gawel's work.

Gawel was a barrel maker. He also made kegs and sturdy wooden buckets needed to bring water from the well. He made clogs from wood. He then bartered his goods for food. He made for me a pair of wooden clogs when my own shoes fell apart. Gawel also made the wooden washtub we used around the house. For barrels and kegs he used soft pinewood, but for clogs he needed the hard wood of a beech or an oak.

In the winter he carried the logs of wood into the hut and cut them with a saw into short stumps the length of the barrel. Piled wood dried in a corner of the room. Wood shavings fell gasping on the clay floor. Even today, the smell of wood reminds me of Stykow.

I was nine years old when I arrived in Stykow. I liked to watch Gawel rip the wood with one blow of his axe. With his legs apart and an axe above his head he looked like a giant from a picture book.

Peeling potatoes by the warm stove, I watched and listened as Gawel made the staves that formed the barrel's wall. I knew by the sound when he chose a suitable stump. I heard how his axe split and chopped the stump along the grain. I watched as he held the piece of wood securely with his large, bony hands, searching for its bends, observing its veins. When he finished chiseling each narrow stave, he put it away until all staves were ready to assemble into the barrel. I came to know the soft cadence and the tangy fragrance of the shaved wood.

In the morning, Agata started the fire, and I cleaned the kitchen. Wood chips danced under my broom. Once or twice I touched Gawel's tools. He had a drawknife, a long, bent, sharp metal tool, with two handles on its ends, with which he chiseled each piece of wood.

Gawel was precise and accurate in everything he did. Every so often he would get up to check that the staves fitted together. Absorbed in his work, he never talked with me. But I could listen and watch. The shrill noise of shaving wood rose and fell. The beat of his hammer resonated in the small room. A soft tap pushed the staves snugly against the metal hoop.

Like a magician, he could change a wooden stump into a pair of perfect clogs. Clogs that sheltered my feet from snow. *Could I ever hold a tool with such confidence?* I was so unhandy, I couldn't even peel a potato thinly. Agata chastised me, but it was useless.

While the potatoes cooked I filled a wooden trough with my chubby peels. Agata watched with disgust. Her small eyes blinked as she turned. "This is no good," she muttered, spreading the skins and sprinkling them with a handful of bran. "So much waste." She lifted the pot steaming with potatoes, poured out the hot liquid, and stirred the cow's fodder. Her heavy legs showed under a long skirt when she bent over the trough.

I took a bucket and drew water from the well. "The cow gets all of the potatoes," Agata said when I returned. She tied a warm shawl across her chest and carried the trough into the barn. It had been a cold winter.

When I finished my chores I sat again to knit and to watch Gawel. I closed my eyes and listened to the beat of his hammer, then opened them just in time to see Gawel pushing the staves against the metal hoop. When all pieces were secured in their grooves, Gawel fastened them together into the hoops, and the barrel was ready to sell or to barter for food.

All that winter while the cow stayed in the barn I knitted. All my things were completely worn out. I knitted sweaters from things at hand.

At home before the war I was prone to illness. In my six short years before the war started, I was in bed with rubella, scarlet fever, whooping cough, measles, and diphtheria. I was always succumbing to all kinds of colds. That was then, before I had left my parents. But now, in the second year on my own, I hardened. Now, running barefoot across a frozen pond without a scarf, a hat, or a coat, I didn't catch cold or didn't notice if I did. In the spring, trying to snap some new leaves for the cow, I walked barefoot to the peat bog knee deep in icy water.

I had almost nothing to wear. My navy-colored skirt, made from a woolen, A-line dress with a trimmed sailor's collar, which I wore when I left home, was wearing out. That skirt, patched and repaired again and again, stayed with me to the end. To lengthen it, I inserted a piece of old fabric in the waistline. I mended the smaller holes and patched the larger ones.

But I had nothing to put on as a top with my skirt. Halinka taught me how to knit, and, using the remnants of woolen sweaters I took from home, I made one large sweater of dappled hue, which I wore with the patched skirt. At first I wore this sweater with the sleeves rolled up, but as I grew it became smaller. My black shoes were long gone, and I went barefoot until Gawel made me the pair of clogs from a piece of wood and a scrap of leather. When I felt cold in winter, I missed my dark-blue winter coat, the coat I had worn over my navy blue dress the night I left home. I remembered that coat well, because of the gold coin sewn into the lining. But I never found the coin, and the coat had quickly disappeared.

In Stykow we lived near the forest, drawing on its resources. We went there to get food and fuel. There was wood for burning in the stove: pinecones, dried twigs, small broken branches. I carried the wood home tied into a blanket. With the bundle over my shoulder, I looked like a clumsy bird on thin legs, walking across the fields.

Early in the summer, we'd gather blueberries. Agata sold some and dried what was left for winter. Later, we searched for mushrooms deep in the woods. We left early in the morning when it was still dark and walked through the dense forest. Here and there a patch of red poisonous mushrooms called *muchomory* tempted me, but I soon learned how to look for good, brown, aromatic mushrooms called *prawdziwki*. *Kozaki*

The Confession

(cossacks), so called for their reddish hats, were also edible but less flavorful. *Maslaki*, moist and slippery to the touch, didn't store well but made a good supper. It was solid dark again when we returned. In the morning we sorted our finds. Pierced, threaded, mushrooms hung above the stove like a brown, aromatic necklace.

A path through the same forest took us to the church. We walked together along the path and along the long stretch of highway afterward. We walked barefoot, carrying along our shoes. I carried my wooden clogs, but with every step I wanted to turn back. I tried to appear peaceful, but I couldn't. Like the other girls I held my prayer book in my right hand with the rosary beads folded around my palm. I protected that book with a clean handkerchief the same way the other girls did, but I was not protected. I knew no way out of my predicament. As I walked, flaxen heads were all around me. I could feel the hot dust of the road under my bare feet the same way they felt it, but my curly hair set me apart. At times I could feel their stares. People would look at me with a searching gaze. In a way my First Communion photo sheltered me from their suspicion. All I had to do now was to pretend. But how could I?

The priest's unwillingness to baptize me put my life into a state of perpetual confusion. Now the dangers were lurking from within and from without. I didn't know what to do, and there wasn't anybody to help me. I was too scared to talk even with Halinka. I don't suppose that the Gavels knew who I was. They never talked with me about it. Except for the priest and the nun from Wola

Rzedzinska, no one ever talked with me about my condition.

Did I really understand that my life was at stake? I knew that I had to hide, but I was only a child, and my task was too hard for me. I knew that I had to do what other children did or be found out quickly as a Jew. People from Stykow must not know I hadn't been baptized; that would immediately give me away.

The priest in Wola Rzedzinska had told me to pretend. I must go on pretending, faking participation in the sacraments of confession and communion. How I wished I could talk with somebody. But I was all alone. Still, I was expected to go to confession and communion as often as the other children from the village. I was supposed to do all that while not even being baptized.

All the time I walked with this never-ceasing pain. That I was not baptized felt like a knife in my heart. I loved Jesus now. This was the only object of affection in my lonely life. Each time I went to church a thorn pierced deeper into my heart.

I didn't know what to do. At first I pretended not to feel well, but my absence at church was always noticed. One morning a neighbor, Stefa, came and began to ask why I wasn't in church the previous Sunday. It was a cold day, and Stefa wore a red kerchief around her head. I went quickly to the barn. I lingered with the cow, afraid to return. I shivered from cold, but I remained in the barn until Stefa left the hut.

I came back to a warm room resounding with Gawel's woodwork. The steady whistle of shaved wood calmed my fears. But now I knew that

The Confession

I must go to confession with the villagers. If I didn't I'd be found out. Yet, I still hesitated. I prayed that I would become ill. I did. I developed a painful boil on the toe of my right foot and couldn't walk for a while. When I finally went to confession, I moved away before approaching the confessional as instructed by the priest from Wola Rzedzinska and only pretended taking the communion. Immersed in their prayers, the parishioners didn't look around. I was also praying, but I knew that what I was doing was wrong. I walked silently from the church. Next Sunday I went to mass and pretended again. I repeated the maneuver and again no one noticed. With time I had become quite skillful in this make-believe ritual, but now and then a thought would return as painful as a cut from a knife: *I am not baptized. I shouldn't be pretending. This is a mortal sin.*

My feeling of uneasiness grew with every trip to the church. I wanted to be baptized. I was afraid that I would go to hell. Each time I knelt in front of the altar I felt the weight of my sins. I prayed and struck my breasts repeating *"Mea culpa, mea culpa, mea maxima culpa,"* but that didn't set me free. I felt like a thief during the procession. My fear grew, and, again, I stopped going to church.

Lent came, the time when going to confession was most important. I still didn't know what to do. Sitting in the field in a newly made furrow I looked at the grubs coming out from the soil to warm in the sun. I watched their slack white trunks softening in the sun and curled my own body. A grub can hide in a furrow. I wanted to be a grub; to lose my visibility and to blend into my surroundings. I drew myself up. I did what I was told to do.

One day I was sitting by the stove when Halinka entered the room. "Next Saturday we will all go to confession." I don't suppose that Halinka knew. She tossed pinecones into the fire and said, "I will take confession, will you?"

"Yes, I will," I said quickly. Halinka put the next bundle of twigs into the stove. They quickly caught fire and gave off more heat. The fire cast a soft glow on Halinka's face, her hair braided neatly in two long strands. I turned my face away from the heat. *What will I do?* I thought in alarm. I sat with Halinka in silence for some time. Nobody should know that I am not baptized. Again, I will do as the others do. Halinka reached to the pail and put more wood into the stove. The small logs burned faster. I thought of the fires of hell. Taking the holy sacrament of confession without being baptized was a mortal sin; I would burn in hell.

That night the smell of hay kept me awake all night. Next to me Halinka's face reflected her clear conscience. She slept soundly without fear of being killed. I thought about burning in hell. I wanted to be baptized. I had to do something. If I continued I would be caught, anyway. *I could tell the priest that I haven't been baptized.* The thought calmed me for a while. I would tell the priest during the confession, and then I would be protected by the sanctity of the sacrament. By now I knew the Catholic Church's doctrines quite well. I felt safe at once. I would confess to the priest, and he would baptize me. Days passed and I didn't change my mind. *I will tell the priest,* I kept repeating to myself.

Every morning, while taking the cow to the pasture, I walked past a small figure of Christ carved in wood. Standing on a crossroad, on a wooden pole, the figure also seemed lonely. Brown, weathered, cut in wood, he seemed to listen and understand. His bent figure expressed compassion. His small face looked at me approvingly. When I knelt to pray I felt stronger about my decision. I stood up and touched the wooden pole with my palm. For a moment I just stood there. I almost felt that he encouraged me to go ahead and tell the priest.

The next Sunday, I went to church determined to confess. When I walked toward the confessional the parishioners had already formed two long lines. They knelt on both sides awaiting their turn to confess. They had walked through the woods a long way to this parish church. Since the last evening they hadn't eaten anything; some hadn't even drunk any water yet. This act of confessing would be followed by an absolution. Then they would form another line awaiting the Holy Communion. The line was long. I waited patiently for my turn.

My open palm met the warm wood of my rosary beads. I kissed the wooden cross of my rosary and thought again about the wooden figure at the crossroads. I could see his eyes looking directly at me. His head, bent to the left, heard my prayers. His half-smiling mouth whispered compassion. I felt his long hands touching my shoulders. I recited my prayers, softly running my fingers over the brown polished beads, and felt consoled with each repetition of *Hail Mary.*

Two hours passed. There were still more than ten people in front of me. I hadn't changed my mind. The church smelled of burned myrrh and old wax. The voices rose high into the heaven. I felt close to the heaven also. An old woman was kneeling behind me loudly repeating her prayers. That was a good sign. Now it was my turn. My face was close to the narrow latticed opening of the small enclosed stall. The priest began his prayer. I crossed myself.

"Father, I haven't been baptized," I whispered confidently.

"In that case you must not take the holy sacrament of confession. I am not giving you absolution."

The priest spoke loudly. I noticed a strange coarseness in his voice, but I couldn't see his face. His hand smelled of soap. It was the same kind of expensive, store-bought scented soap used by the priest in Wola Rzedzinska. The smell reminded me of the hand of the priest who refused to baptize me. Without a word I walked away.

For a moment I felt assured that no one had noticed what had happened at the confessional. I could still hear their voices reciting the litany. I continued my prayers, trying to behave as though I was going to communion. I remembered what the priest said, but I had to pretend. Taking advantage of the crowded church I was going to pretend again.

I stepped into the nave to go up the altar and moved closer, ready to approach the communion rail. Three rows of worshipers were kneeling awaiting their turns. With my heart pounding, I knelt praying. I did not intend to take the communion. The next row of parishioners moved closer to the pulpit. They kept their hands folded, and they looked down. *Nobody will notice,* I thought, approaching the pulpit.

But I was unaware of a short, earnest woman who kept a careful watch over me. It was the same woman who had knelt behind me awaiting confession. The same woman who overheard the priest's verdict at the confessional. Now, kneeling with the other parishioners awaiting communion, the old woman watched. Perhaps she feared that a sinner was going to commit a sacrilege and that as a soldier of God she must defend him from desecration. She yelled, "Father, this girl didn't receive absolution!"

Paralyzed by her screaming voice, I didn't know what to do. Somehow I managed to bend down; then I slowly turned toward the sacristy. The parishioners were still praying, taking part in the communion. Out of their sight I began to run. I didn't stop until I reached the forest. I spent the night there. In the rustle of the trees I heard the shout again: "She didn't receive absolution!" And it was true; I didn't. I disobeyed my father's command and revealed my secret. I didn't get help; instead, I was singled out in the crowd of people.

All night long I heard the woman's scream across the crowded church. I felt deserted and betrayed. I kept hoping that nobody from Stykow had noticed what had happened to me, but I knew that they had. I ran through the forest. Still thinking of her, trying to escape, I cut through the thick underbrush. I felt my face stiffen even as my body was moving. I imagined the peasants searching for me and stopped, too scared to go on. I continued, startled by my heartbeat; loud, fast, violent. Convinced that they could hear its pounding I lowered my body and hid in the dense underbrush. Then, I heard my teeth drumming.

I felt a stab in my back. It was only a broken branch, but I envisioned myself being captured, and dread filled my chest. My hands were shaking again. I seized a pinecone and held it tight.

I crouched behind a tree, waiting. I didn't dare to move; tense, stiffened by the expectation of what was coming. Far in the east side, where I ran from, I heard a sound. I didn't know what it was, and a chill ran down my spine. I imagined people running with pitchforks, axes, hammers. *They will kill me now.* I jumped up, ready to run away. I stopped. I had nowhere to go. *They will find me and turn me in.* Retreating I felt my back cold against the tree. I didn't want to cry. I stuffed my two clenched fists into my mouth and listened, but the sound didn't recur.

I can't cry; I have to hide somewhere where no one will find me. From afar I heard a goose cackle. I listened for a moment in disbelief. Geese cackling, which once filled my heart with fear, now calmed me down. I stood and hugged the tree. I felt my body trembling as it pressed against the trunk. Upright I regained my composure. I rested my head on the tree trunk and put my arms around it. The bark was rough but warm; behind a hard crust the tree was gentle.

I touched the coarse bark. I promised myself to be smarter now. *I shall never admit that I am Jewish. I shall not reveal who I am. This way I shall be safe.* I listened again. I was still hugging the pine tree. I ran my hands up and down the bark. My wits were catching up. *I must find my way out. I can't go back to Stykow. Where should I go?* Hearing the geese cackling again, I recalled Maryla and Hucisko.

On a wagon taking us both from the train station, Maryla had shown me the way to her sister's hut in Hucisko. "Can you see the small hut by the woods? My sister Zosia lives there. Try to remember your way to Hucisko." Maryla cupped her hands over a cigarette when the driver turned into the narrow road. They smoked in silence, and I watched politely. When the driver stopped the horse and left us for a moment, Maryla squashed the cigarette and turned to me. "If you need to, you can go to Hucisko and stay there with Zosia. Try to remember the way."

It was a short visit in Hucisko then, as Maryla visited with her sister only for one day before leaving me in Stykow with the Gawels. But I remembered. I started walking through the woods, guided by the sounds of the geese. I made my way to the village and hid in a haystack until night came. The next morning I found my way to Hucisko.

Ja,Maria Oraczowa zamieszkała w Krakowie-Płaszowie ul.Boczna-Sarmacka nr.14,oświadczam co następuje :w roku 1941 wzięłam pod opiekę dziewczynkę narodowości żydowskiej/Miriam Winter, urodzoną w Łodzi/ a przewiezioną do Ożarowa k/ Warszawy z getta warszawskiego;reszta rodziny dziewczynki prawdopodobnie zginęła; dziecko ukrywałam z narażaniem własnego życia zarówno przed Niemcami jak i przed współpracującymi z nimi Ukraińcami i "mongołami" ; sypiałyśmy pod mostem,w kopkach siana i w zbożu szukając bezpiecznego schronienia podczas wielokrotnego dziesiątkowania ludności polskiej; wobec bezpośredniego zagrożenia prześladowanej przez okupantów dziewczynki- kilkanaście razy zmieniałam Jej miejsce pobytu; spośród osób ,które najbardziej pomogły mi w Jej przechowaniu pragnę wymienić księdza proboszcza parafii Wola Rzędzińska w diecezj. Tarnowskiej;w roku 1944 dziecko zostało ochrzczone,otrzymało imiona Bronisława-Maria i zapisane na nazwisko Dudek w aktach parafialnych kościoła św. Marcina we Lwowie

Po roku 1945 dziecko wychowywało w mojej rodzinie,a następni w Państwowych Domach Dziecka w Szczecinie i Koszalinie.

Wiarogodność powyższych danych potwierdza mój mąż- Ryszard Oracz zamieszkały pod tym samym adresem.

24/XI. 1961r.

Hucisko

Hucisko was smaller than Stykow. Maryla's sister Zosia lived there with her four children and her husband, Bartek. Bartek was a thin, placid man with two missing front teeth that muddled his speech. He always seemed lethargic in contrast with his wife, Zosia, who was a tall, dark-haired woman with a strong, furrowed face and burning eyes.

Like the Gawels, the Barteks also lived in one room. I slept in the attic again; Zosia's children slept together in a narrow bed that stood by the wall near the woodstove. Every morning when Zosia started a fire and the light shone upward on her strong, bony face, she looked unreal.

Zosia was a fortune-teller and spoke with a harsh voice. People in the village thought she was a witch. They came to hear their fortunes told from a deck of cards. They visited at dark hours and brought bread, or potatoes, or beans. Occasionally somebody brought eggs, which Zosia would cook on the top of the stove. A deck of cards, spread waiting on the wooden table, was like a book, unread.

I was ten years old when I arrived in Hucisko. Again, as in the other places, I said that my mother worked in Krakow. Again, I did my chores. The cow that grazed on the narrow path between someone's fields had to be watched all the time. At night, after putting the cow into the barn, I would warm myself at the fire and watch Zosia's maneuvers. A girl would come and tell Zosia about her sorrows, and Zosia would quickly search for the right card.

"That's you, and that king is a mature man. He likes you. Do you know him?" Zosia would then listen to the girl's musing and deftly retell her story, inserting low-pitched expressions like "in the moonlight," "at the night's fall," "thinking of you," "what the heart desires," as if she read all this from the old deck of cards.

When I finished my chores I could read. That summer in Hucisko I read books borrowed from Basia, a stout, middle-aged woman whose future Zosia foretold repeatedly. I remember Basia's first visit. I had been reading outside until it was so dark that I couldn't see anything. Back inside the hut I reached for the kerosene lamp; the shade was covered with black soot. I cleaned the black glass with a handful of straw, but when I lit the lamp, Zosia said:

"Don't waste kerosene or we'll have to sit in the dark in winter. Start the fire and sweep the floor, Basia is coming."

As I finished sweeping Basia entered and handed Zosia a loaf of bread. Her shawl fell on her shoulder, and she looked frightened to me. Zosia wiped a wooden stool with her apron.

"You sit here," she said, touching Basia's braid.

Basia smoothed her dark, long skirt and sat waiting, while Zosia placed a wooden box in the center of the table. With her long index finger Zosia drew an imaginary circle around the box. Then, she knocked twice on the carved lid, opened the box, and took out a deck of cards. They smelled of chamomile. Zosia seemed unaffected, but I knew how intensely she watched her visitors. Presently, she lit a candle and searched for the queen of hearts.

"That's you," she said in a rasping voice. Then, with a bold forward gesture, she set her cards down.

"Cut them."

Basia's face flushed; she moved the deck nervously and quickly clasped her hands. Zosia spread the cards in three rows, murmuring:

"What's lurking in the dark, what shall come, what has happened before."

I noticed how skillfully Zosia used the light to get hold of Basia's feelings. Frequently, she moved the candle before rearranging the cards. In the glow, her face looked unreal. The long shadow moved on the wall.

"You are waiting for someone to come," she said slowly, but Basia was silent. Zosia watched her dimpled face for a sign of approval; finding none, she lowered her eyes.

"I see clear water . . ."

TRAINS

"Choose three cards," Zosia said, pointing to the cards spread in a circle again. Her face was solemn now.

"Make a wish," she whispered.

She waited, but Basia only moved her lips without uttering a sound. I put more wood into the fire. Zosia covered her eyes with her palms. I felt the silence in the room. Only the fire was hissing. Once more, Zosia gathered the cards.

"Think about something you want." She shuffled, set the cards again, and let Basia uncover a king of hearts.

"Now, think about him and cut three times toward your heart." Only then, Zosia declared:

"He loves you."

Basia's bosom moved faster; her round face lighted.

"Don't thank me," Zosia warned her, while Basia tied her shawl across her chest and walked out.

Again and again, Basia came to learn about her future. I found myself waiting for her visits. Often she had a book for me to read. When night came I drew the bench closer to the fire and read. Zosia scolded me for reading when there was still work to be done. The lampshade was sooty again, but I was afraid to clean it now. How I wished to be as obedient as Jadzia, the good-hearted girl I read about.

Another woman noticed my reading and brought me a book that lingered in my memory. Amicis's *From Appenines to Andes* was a compelling story of a boy separated from his mother. The boy's loneliness moved me to tears. Searching for her he went alone across the ocean and finally found her in the Andes of South America. At night, I ruminated about the boy's adventures. *Could I be as brave as he was?*

But I did not admit to any similarities with my own life. As if my previous life did not exist, I lived from day to day, without looking back.

Only once, reading *Stern*, a magazine published by Germans, did I think about my father. There was a story about a boy who found a wounded man in the woods, not knowing that it was, in fact, his father. *Would I recognize my own father?* I didn't know. I thought that I still knew his name, but I wasn't sure anymore.

Once I cleaned the forester's room and noticed a pile of books.

"Could I borrow one?" I asked.

"I don't have anything suitable for children, but take whatever you want," he replied. "Just bring it back."

The forester had travel and adventure books, and I dreamed of going far away where *The Last of the Mohicans* roamed on his horse through the forest.

Early each morning I took the cow to the pasture. I held the rope, but, in fact, it was I who was tied to the cow. Her name was Lyska (Baldie), a name inspired by the white-colored spot on her head. I cleansed Lyska with straw, covered her with a blanket on cold evenings, and fed her during the winter.

This morning was pleasant. Mist was still in the air after last night's rain and the grass felt soft under my bare feet. I let Lyska choose her pace; she walked slowly. Time and again, she chomped a mouthful of grass. On the next pathway a peasant girl about my age was turning cartwheels.

I walked heavily. Even my clothes were bearing me down. Stick in hand, walking after the cow, covered with a ragged blanket, I didn't bounce. I had outgrown all my clothes. I barely remembered what I had taken along when I left my parents. My navy blue skirt, the only reminder of my normal life, was completely worn out. I had mended it once more, but now, by my third year on my own, that skirt was falling apart faster than I could put another patch over the holes.

My urbane way of speaking was long gone. In 1941 when I went into hiding my grammar and vocabulary marked me as a city girl. Now, in 1943, I used the same peasant dialect as any girl from the village.

Food was scarce. We ate cabbage with potatoes or cabbage with beans. Zosia had a few chickens, but eggs were like money. One egg bought a sewing needle, three a pencil, five a notebook. Nonetheless, I didn't starve. In the villages where I was hiding there was always something to eat. Cabbage was always cooking on the stove.

Germans rarely entered those villages. The region had poor soil, so there wasn't much food to confiscate. But for me, it was easy to satisfy my hunger in the fields. In the early summer, I'd suck an unripe wheat spikelet, the same way village children did. The juice from young wheat had a soothing milky taste. Later, I'd gather fallen wild pears under a tall tree. The small round fruit, hard and bitter when picked up, softened in straw into a mushy texture and a sweet, figlike taste, one remembered from home.

Hucisko

In the fall, when digging began, the peasants would pull up heaps of potatoes. At night, children would start a bonfire to bake what was left in the fields after digging.

Earlier in my hiding, in 1941, I had recalled *czulent,* a baked potato dish, when I smelled for the first time the burned aroma of a field-baked potato. Then, I couldn't stop thinking of home. Tears filled my eyes. Climbing a ladder on my way to the attic where I slept, I stopped to watch the children. Smoke wafted low from their fires. The cinders glowed in the dark. The smell was all around me. The whole world smelled like *czulent.* Even the hay in the attic smelled like *czulent.* I sank deep into the hay and cried myself to sleep.

But now, in Hucisko, in the fall of 1943, I stopped thinking about my past. I didn't cry anymore. I didn't try to talk to anybody. I was more careful now. After my failed confession I kept watch all the time. I lived only in the present.

The days went by. I didn't notice. As I moved from village to village, my days were alike. At daybreak I took the cow to graze. Mute, dumb, silent, I spent all my time with the cow. But I felt lonely, isolated from the past, desperate for affection, with no one to comfort me. Were there people to care for me? I couldn't tell.

Once, after church, I joined some girls sitting on the grass. I was drawn toward their laughter like a moth flitting about the light, but they stopped laughing as I approached. Shut off by their silence, I walked away. I often thought that things would have been different if I had somebody, anybody. If I could belong. But I didn't. My curly black hair was proof of my guilt.

TRAINS

In spring the peasants whitewashed the wooden walls of their huts. In summer they grew pink cosmos, red gladioli, and white tall malvas in the narrow patch in front of their houses. The fields were gold, red, and blue, with cornflowers and poppies blooming in the rye. How I wished I could change the color of my hair.

Once I gathered some cornflowers in the rye field and braided a wreath. "I am a flower of strength," I said to Lyska, but she went on grazing as if she didn't really believe me. Removing my crown I noticed a ladybug walking across the blue petals. Her Polish name is *Boza Krowka* (God's little cow). I held the reddish, black-dotted bug in the center of my palm and with an upward motion threw her to the sky:

> Boza krowko lec to nieba
> przynies mi kawalek chleba.
>
> Fly to the heaven god's little cow
> and fetch me a piece of bread.

With these words I moved my palm gently upward to let my ladybug know that it was safe to fly. Then, I closed my eyes, waiting. I didn't starve. I waited for magic—like Basia . . .

My own life was now as tattered as my rags were. I didn't think anymore about my life as it once was. Sometimes an unexpected association moved me to tears, but I learned to conceal my feelings; I put a smile on my face like a ragged patch on my woolen skirt.

Once, coming back from the fields, I saw a child playing with his mother's chin and felt a sharp pain like the cut of a fine wire. I stood motionless watching them. The woman sat in a doorway. The little boy on her lap was less than a year old. The child touched her face. Moving his small fingers from her chin, to her lips, up to the tip of her nose until he touched the hollows of her eyes, he examined her face. I didn't cry. The woman closed her eyes, letting him explore. Repeatedly, she kissed his fingers when they touched her lips. Each time I heard the loud kissing sound, I felt a choking in my throat. She didn't stop him even when he twisted her nose.

I felt a movement of the rope. Lyska jerked me along. I turned at once and patted her neck. Then I marched resolutely toward Zosia's hut.

But at night I had frightening dreams. Days were harsher, too. I was scratching my head all the time. Having lice in my hair made my life more like that of other children in the village. Sometimes we used a thick comb with long and narrow dark brown teeth to remove them. But it was easier to spot and to kill lice by hand. One day Aniela, Zosia's daughter, sat by me on a doorstep. Warmed by the sun, a louse walked across her blonde hair. My hair was also full of lice. Small, sandy grains of lice's eggs shone prominently on my black hair.

Once, on a hot day, gadflies attacked Lyska in the pasture. Lyska lay in a meadow with her rope firmly attached to her short stout neck. I stood by holding the rope. I liked to feel in my palm its rough ridged texture of the rope. When I held the rope tight, without wavering, I was in control.

Suddenly, I heard a harsh, infuriated buzz. A moment later a few gadflies gathered on Lyska's back. She bellowed and tried to swat them away with her tail, but the flies sat unmoved. Soon, more gadflies buzzed around her like airplanes before invasion. They landed on her golden brown fur in a swarm, gnawing, stinging, biting at her. Lyska slapped her tail to chase them away, but they only stung deeper. Helplessly she wagged her tail. Nothing helped. For a while I tried to hold the rope, but she kicked, and I lost it. Barefoot, trying to catch hold of the rope, I cut my feet against a sharp stone.

Lyska's hide was covered with dark, grayish, stinging gadflies. She slapped again. She raised her head, wailing loudly. She couldn't be still. I tried to help her but retreated when her wet tail hit me hard about my face. Once more, she halted, and I stooped clumsily. Unyielding I held the rope. All of a sudden she jumped up, pulling the rope, but I caught the end again and held it tight. A moment later, Lyska pulled the rope away and started to run. I caught the rope, trying to steer her toward the pasture, but she bolted and raced toward the barn.

That night, I had a frightening dream. I dreamed that someone had discovered my secret. I wanted to run away, but my legs wouldn't move. I wanted to scream but couldn't utter any sound.

Hucisko

If I wasn't in the pasture with Lyska, I worked in the fields. When a task was too hard I did something else, but I worked as a farmhand in every one of my hiding places. Life in the village revolved in a cycle of crop and root. The peasants lived from the fields and needed every pair of hands. Rye flourished in their poor soil. They also grew millet, oats, potatoes, groats, beets, cabbage, beans, and flax.

I was helpful when it was time to gather flax. Linseeds sown in spring produced long thin twigs. In the fall, we pulled out the matured twigs, now brown and hardened, and tied them into small bunches. The smell of flax permeated the air. We soaked bunches of flax in the stream to soften the fibers. We spread untied flax thinly on the grass to dry out in the sun. Then, to break up the dried twigs, we hit them in a fast, continuous motion. The shards flew away with the wind. Finally, with a metal tool that lay on the floor like a giant hairbrush, we combed out the flax. Only then was the combed flax ready to put on a distaff to spin. The shards, called *pazdzierze*, gave their name to *pazdziernik*, the month of October.

Winters set the spindles whirling. Old women sat side by side around the room. The girls were knitting. We didn't have wool, so everything was made from flax: socks, sweaters, even mittens.

TRAINS

Zosia showed me how to make socks with a set of five needles, and I knitted in her hut. The hard linen thread was difficult to manipulate, but I persisted. When the stockings were ready, Zosia gave me another skein of flax.

Sun shone through the frozen window, reflecting the ice etchings. I looked at the window and spun stories from the contours of the ice. I imagined a castle and a girl inside. The walls of the castle were transparent, and everybody could see her there. But she couldn't get out.

"You didn't sweep the floor," said Zosia. I took the broom; Zosia gathered her cards. Alone with my broom I looked at the frozen window. Inside the castle was a girl in a pleated skirt. Sweeping, I thought about a knight on a narrow pathway. The knight looked at the castle and the girl inside. My broom changed into a horse. I stepped across the broomstick, galloping away.

Summer came. When I went to the woods to get firewood, a broken bough stood for a sword. When I went to the fields, I imagined myself on horseback. The road curved, and I stood in front of a castle. The girl in the pleated skirt was still there.

At night, I imagined a knight riding his horse through the fields. He searched for a way into the castle, but a ragged straw man chased him away. I sucked a rye spike still too young to harvest and imagined the knight, sitting tall in a saddle on a chestnut horse. I saw him fight the straw man, or the monster, I wasn't sure which.

My health worsened; I had painful boils on my feet again. To cure them Zosia applied small leaves of a weed called *babka* (*Plantago major*). The cool touch of the crushed fleshy leaf gave temporary relief, but the boils didn't heal until Zosia punctured them with a needle, letting the fluid out.

About that time Maryla came from Lwow. She visited her sister several times while I stayed in Hucisko, but her visits were always short. I still called her *Mamusia*.

Returning from the woods with an armful of firewood, I saw Maryla entering Zosia's hut. I ran back with the twigs scratching my face.

"Mamusia!"

I wanted to hug her, but she walked away. Her tall boots stepped with a hollow sound against the clay floor. "Mamusia," I repeated softly, but she didn't touch me.

She looked different. Maryla had let her hair down, and her strong face, barely lighted by the kerosene lamp, looked similar to Zosia's. Both sisters were tall, with strong profiles and dark, straight hair.

Still booted, Maryla cracked open a box of cigarettes. Early on, when we first met, Maryla smoked thin, long, filtered cigarettes called *Damskie* (ladies' choice). I remember Maryla's bony fingers holding a cigarette. Then, she held a thin filtered cigarette between her middle and her index fingers. Now she curled her five fingers tightly over a short butt. In 1941, when I first met Maryla, she wore tailored suits with short skirts and jackets with padded shoulders. Now, in 1943, Maryla arrived in Hucisko clad in beige gabardine breeches and high, black, leather boots.

I drew nearer. Maryla leaned back, extending her strong legs.

"Help me take off my boots."

Crouched in front of her I pulled on her tightly fitted leather boot.

"Try harder."

I pulled with all my strength, but Maryla's boot still clung to her leg.

"Try again."

I pulled with both hands, as hard as I could, until at last, I tumbled on my back still holding Maryla's shiny boot above my head.

From a red velvet sack Maryla removed shoe polish and an old woolen sock. Zosia filled a bowl with hot water, and Maryla soaked her feet. Polishing her boots I noticed the strong smell of her cigarettes. The cigarette box had an image of a discus thrower and blue letters, *Sport*, printed on its cover. Before lighting her cigarette, Maryla tapped it gently against the box.

"Why do you do that?" asked Bartek, who was also a heavy smoker.

"For good luck," said Maryla.

On her next visit, Maryla rolled her own cigarettes using tobacco and thin white tissue paper. Bartek rolled his tobacco in newspaper scraps. Zosia grew a few tobacco plants in her potato field, which was illegal because the government had a monopoly over alcohol and tobacco.

One day Maryla took me to a peasant's house to buy pork. Just a week before, Zosia had punctured my boils and my feet were still hurting me badly, but I didn't want to refuse. I wanted to be near her. The peasant had just slaughtered a pig. Maryla bought some kielbasa and a slab of pork fat. After the transaction, we carried Maryla's suitcase together. Maryla rubbed her ears, but she didn't touch me.

Back in the hut, Maryla melted the pork fat, and the smell was all over the place. At once Zosia's children surged home. The smell excited them. Inside, they swarmed around the iron stove. Except for this one vivid scene, I barely remember Zosia's children. They kept to themselves.

In the summer of 1944 I was eleven years old. Just before the harvest Maryla came again to Hucisko and moved me to another village, Ranizow, I think. I remember what I did there, but I don't recall people except Jadzia, a stout woman who taught me how to cut millet with a sickle. As in the other villages, I worked. Another pair of hands was always needed. Someone had to take the cow to the pasture and watch her all the time. Walking the narrow path between the fields, I held the rope tight; otherwise, the cow would crumple someone's field or feed on someone's wheat or potatoes. I wasn't strong enough to milk the cow, but I cleansed her with straw, covered her with a blanket on cold evenings, and fed her during the winter.

Year-round, the peasants worked in the fields, and I worked with them. Reaping was a man's work. The scythe moved in half-circles in step with the walking man who cut the ripe spears of rye in an even, steady motion. As it fell slowly on the field, the rye produced a sound like a litany of voices in a crowded church. Behind the man with the scythe walked a woman gathering the freshly cut crop, stopping only to bind it with a straw band. Everything belonged together; the movements and the sounds resonated in oneness: the woman walking slowly behind the reaper, even the occasional cry of a child lying in the field with a handful of poppy seed tied in a piece of cloth to put him to sleep. I didn't belong. I was like the brightly colored weed in a uniform field of even sameness.

Rye stock dug sharply into my bare feet when, after the harvest, I walked the cow into the stubble. The cow's name was Krasna. While Krasna grazed I gleaned the rye spikes left in the field. Back in the hut I removed the grains, but I wasn't strong enough to grind rye, which required the use of stone grinders, called *zarna.*

Zarna consisted of two large stone circles, like two car tires one stuck on top of the other. When the Germans closed the mills the peasants again used this ancient device. A handful of rye was ground into a coarse flour between those two stones. Jadzia was strong. I could barely reach the wooden handle.

"Move aside," said Jadzia, turning the stone with ease. To make bread, Jadzia mixed the coarse flour with water strained from boiling potatoes, added a starter that she kept in a clay pot, effortlessly kneaded the soft thick dough, and let it rest in a warm room. Later, Jadzia shaped a round loaf, placed it on a wooden shovel, spread a horse-radish leaf underneath, moistened the surface of the loaf, and shoved her rye bread into a hot oven. Soon, Jadzia's hut smelled like a loaf of bread. All around the rye loaf shone a crunchy brown crust. On the bottom crust the horse-radish leaf carved deep veins into the bread. As in the other villages, I cut oats and millet by using a sickle. Jadzia noticed that my work could be improved.

"Grab as much straw as you can." She demonstrated while I mimicked her motions. Her large hand held about fifty spikes. It looked easy, but my short fingers couldn't reach around.

"Close your palm."

I held barely a dozen spikes.

"This way you'll never finish; grab as much as you can."

I grabbed a handful of millet.

"Hold it tight."

"Now, swing a half-circle, just so . . ."

She cut off a thick sheaf; the golden grains shook like a feather. I swayed with my right hand and cut off the tops. She corrected me again:

"Bend lower, grab where your ankles are."

I wasn't as strong as Jadzia, but I learned eagerly and worked as hard as she did.

In a similar manner, Jadzia showed me how to use a wooden *stomp* to remove chaff from the grains of oats and millet. The *stomp* was another old farm tool. Made entirely of wood, it moved up and down like a seesaw. I would put a small amount of grain into the wooden bowl and stamp the wooden hammer into the bowl until the chaff was separated from the grain.

Later in Ranizow I slept in a barn and had frightening dreams again. Below, men were threshing rye. Asleep, I heard the rhythmic beat and dreamed that they crushed me with their flails.

TRAINS

I woke up, touching my shoulders. It was only a dream; I was safe. But the next night the flails banged again at the heap of rye, and I dreamed about a monster climbing the ladder to fetch me from my bundle of straw.

A knight held a sword in his hand, ready to fight the monster, but he fell down. Then, I saw a galloping horse with his mouth foaming. The knight marched toward his horse, but he couldn't catch him; his heavy armor pulled him down. The rhythmic beat of the horse's hooves grew louder, and the knight fell down again. I saw his half-open mouth, his frightened eyes. I heard the beat of the galloping horse and woke up. Below, men blasted at the straw.

Late in the summer of 1944 the Germans retreated from that part of Rzeszowszczyzna.

The Front Comes

Elsie, an eleven-year-old, has read about the Holocaust and wants to interview a survivor for a class project. I was Elsie's age when Maryla took me back to Lwow. I look at this girl with a notebook. Her hair is as blond as safety, and I feel again as lonely as a girl with a valise in a crowded terminal. "I am the only one from my entire family who survived," I tell Elsie. "I don't even know how they were killed." Elsie asks, "Why didn't you try to find your family?" I tried once, during a school trip to Warsaw in 1951. Before entering the Red Cross station, I made sure nobody noticed me going there. A woman was sitting behind a glass window, and I gave her a small piece of paper with large block letters. For the first time since parting with my family I wrote my real name, Miriam Winter. I asked whether anybody had looked for me. The woman checked her files and said, "No, no one did." That was all.

Why do I keep comparing myself with Elsie? We are from different worlds. My own puberty came late. Undernourished childhood left me underdeveloped when girls my own age turned into women. Childhood? Even the word seems ironic.

TRAINS

Wrapped in the folds of the old blanket, I was just a girl with a cow.

By early summer in 1944, the Red Army advanced, and on July 27 the Germans retreated from Lwow. Soon after, Ranizow was liberated. I was in the pasture with the cow, Krasula, who had black skin with white patches. Far on the horizon were the black contours of the forest. Behind the forest the troops were already fighting, but the villagers hoped for the front line to pass them by. Today Krasula didn't graze but moaned and stood motionless. I began to pet Krasula. This often worked. Feeling my hand on her back Krasula would begin to graze again. This time, Krasula raised her head, moaned again, and lay down. I heard shots. Gunfire intensified. It was some while before I realized that those were artillery shots. I heard an explosion, a tumult of voices, and then silence. I forced Krasula to stand, and we went back to the village.

It was now obvious that the front line was coming to the village, and I joined the peasants who hid in the ditches. We sat deep in mud. When the shooting ceased for a while we dug deeper to form primitive trenches. After the Germans retreated, the peasants returned to their huts. The war was over for them, but not for me. I don't recall how I felt, as I walked back.

Even before the front line came to Ranizow the villagers knew about the stocks of ammunition held by the Germans in the forest. Every Sunday they walked by those German stocks sheltered from view, hidden under the trees, camouflaged by makeshift roofs covered with sod to resemble grass. To a pilot flying over the forest it looked like a pasture but those were stocks of ammunition piled neatly in a cube the size of a small hut and tucked away from sight.

Nobody guarded those piles anymore. As soon as the gunfire ceased, people went to the forest, returning with German woolen blankets, military coats, and black leather boots. Later young boys went into the forest. Stas, a boy of thirteen, was killed there trying to disassemble a hand grenade that he found. When he failed to open it by pulling the green pin on its side he took a stone and began pounding. The grenade exploded in his face, and Stas was killed instantaneously. When the other boys came to look for Stas, they found his remains scattered around a tree.

Shortly after the front line passed Ranizow, Maryla arrived and took me to live with her once more in Lwow. She brought a jar of strawberry jam in her brown valise. Before we left I went with Maryla to get *Samogon*, also called *Bimber*. A peasant set up his moonshine equipment in the forest and started a fire in a makeshift oven. We spent the night waiting for the liquor brewed from potatoes to drip through a rubber pipe into a kettle.

TRAINS

When we boarded the train and elbowed our way to a crowded compartment, Maryla's large valise was filled with those bottles of *Samogon*.

Return to Lwow

It is spring now, and the soil is waiting. I dig holes into the slope of my garden for dark corms of canna that will bloom later, in August. Today is Wednesday, May 18, 1994, but my thoughts spring to Lwow, where bright red canna grew in front of Maryla's apartment on Academicki Square in the fall of 1944. With Lwow and Ranizow free from the Germans, I didn't have to hide anymore, and so Maryla brought me back to live with her.

I left a village and returned to a city. Not to Lodz, where I was born and lived with my parents before the war: I went to Lwow with Maryla, and I called her Mother: *Mamusia*. Mamusia changed my last name from Kowalska to Dudek and introduced me as her daughter. Even after we parted, I kept that false name, Marysia (Maria) Dudek. Still hiding behind a Christian name, Maria, I didn't admit that I was Jewish.

I didn't look for my family. I didn't try to find out what had happened to them. As if I didn't want them to live even in my memory, I didn't search. I should have looked everywhere; I should have crawled and sifted and asked everyone; I should have flattened myself to the blood-soaked earth. But I didn't. It was time to bend down looking for my other missing beads, but I did nothing, and I remained incomplete like a broken necklace. And so, I survived the hunt, but emerged frozen, with no identity of my own.

I should have shouted out, "My name is Miriam Winter!" But I didn't come out of my hiding, and so no one called me by my real name.

———

The sky looked gray through the window as I rode the train with Maryla. I descended from the train onto the platform and walked among the rushing passengers, small, lost in the crowd. At one moment, pushed against the wall by the mass of people, I stood waiting for Maryla, who watched her step so as not to break any of the bottles that filled her old valise. I wanted to cry, but, determined not to upset Maryla, I raised my head and looked around instead. On the walls of the terminal hung signs printed with characters I couldn't read.

Lwow, liberated from the Germans, was now full of Soviet soldiers. Large posters and slogans were everywhere. Enigmatic signs covered the walls of the terminal. I saw posters urging workers to join the army or to work better. I tried to decipher some words. Not knowing the Cyrillic alphabet, I couldn't read the slogans printed underneath, but I could guess the meaning of the posters depicting men in uniforms.

Return to Lwow

Passing through the door of the railroad station, I again felt lost in the mass of people. When we came out onto the street in Lwow and pushed to get to the tramway, I saw Soviet soldiers in olive green uniforms. The Russian language had a familiar sound, and I could understand some words. I heard the word *vodka* and recalled the content of the brown valise.

Free at last, I returned to Maryla's apartment. I could greet my neighbors. I could open the doors without danger of being found out. I could go to a store to buy milk. Once more in Lwow, I could walk the street and go back to the apartment on Akademicki Square, and no one would tell that a Jewish girl hid in the building. I could run up and down the stairs without fear. I was free, and I was alive. But I remained dead inside. I had almost no memories of my former life.

I don't know why Maryla changed my birth date from June 2, 1933, to September 17, 1937. Today I think that she didn't want to appear old, and so she made me younger. In brain and body a girl of eleven, I had to pretend to be seven years old. I didn't look that young. No one believed me, and I had to keep explaining. It was ridiculous. It added one more lie. I dwelled suspended between facts, belonging nowhere, having nobody, frozen in limbo.

———

The streetcar stopped near Academicki Square in the center of Lwow. We crossed the square, and I noticed a flower bed with tall red canna in full bloom. The entryway smelled of vodka. The valise was too heavy for us to carry upstairs. Luckily, the janitor showed up. His name was Witek. He was taller than Maryla, and his lanky frame reminded me of Gawel. Walking briskly toward us, he kept his hands in his pockets. He was wearing a brown visored cap.

"Let me take it," he said, smiling. His face lit up with this smile. Inside her apartment, Maryla poured vodka into small crystal glasses. Witek took off his cap, exposing prominent ears and short-cropped hair.

"Na zdrowie." He raised his glass, toasting Maryla.

I went to the window and looked down. In the courtyard a little boy played with his dog. He pranced back and forth, ignoring my stare. I recalled that in 1941, when I stayed in Maryla's apartment, the children called me *Zydowa*. Now I didn't have to hide. But I was still afraid to admit to being Jewish.

"They say that Lwow will soon be given to the Soviets," said Witek. Maryla gave him an angry look.

After he left I helped Maryla to unpack her brown valise. She set the bottles on the kitchen table.

Another departure and another arrival that didn't help me return to my past. I still didn't go to school. In Lwow I helped Maryla sell vodka on the black market. Constantly moving, disoriented, uncared for, disconnected, I was now thrust from a village into a city without warning. From a girl with a cow I changed into a street peddler.

Early in the afternoon we would both arrive at the marketplace and walk in the crowd. Maryla needed me to watch for NKVD, the Soviet secret police, who often arrived unexpectedly. Vodka was in the blood of the city, and I helped Maryla sell vodka to the Russian soldiers.

In the market in Lwow, Maryla wore beige gabardine trousers, shiny black high boots, and a long beige trench coat. On cold days she covered her head with a red beret. She kept a bottle in each pocket as she walked among the crowd, repeating in a loud whisper, "*Vodka, nastojaczna vodka.*" *Nastoyashchaya* is a Russian word meaning real, genuine, "the real McCoy." The Polish black marketeers altered the foreign word and called it *nastojaczna* to let the soldiers know that the product was first quality. Maryla's own mixture wasn't genuine, but the soldiers were buying anyway.

Later on, Maryla would buy a large bottle of *spiritus*, "pure grain alcohol," and make her own mixture for sale. At night, I helped Maryla get her bottles ready for the market. I watched Maryla mixing water with alcohol. She filled the bottles, I inserted the corks, and she fastened the cork deep into the neck of each bottle. Next, Maryla held a red stick of sealing wax over the flame of a candle, and when its tip melted, she quickly sealed the corks in the bottle necks, letting the red wax flow down the bottles. Then, Maryla placed a counterfeit stamping mark on her dining room table and dipped each bottle into the stamp. At the end each bottle looked as if it had been officially sealed. The government had a monopoly over alcohol, and what Maryla was doing was illegal.

TRAINS

Every day we went to the market, where Maryla stuck a bottle into each pocket of her trench coat. She kept the remainder inside her brown bag, which was still too heavy to lug around. I stood in a corner watching the bag and observing the market.

"Nastojaczna," Maryla would whisper to a passing soldier. Eager to get vodka the soldiers usually paid and left, but some lingered longer. Sometimes Maryla brought a Russian soldier along to the apartment. I heard their laughter late at night. They drank vodka and sang sad, wailing, Russian songs. One "Wolga, Wolga," still lingers in my heart.

On some mornings, on the other side of Maryla, a man lay in the large bed. Oleg was one of them. His broad face was framed with curly blond hair. Others' faces looked different, uniforms alike.

I remember a man sitting on a wooden crate nearby me in the market. He was wearing a striped vest, but he was without a topcoat. He sat with his legs bent, feet turned inward, the wrist of his right hand clutched tightly in his left hand. He sat on an empty crate with his head bent down and his eyes closed, his long fingers and his thin body clenched in sadness.

I shivered in the November wind. Instead of laboring in farm fields I worked in a big city marketplace without as much as a change of clothing. I didn't have a coat but couldn't cover myself with a blanket as I did in the village.

Once, a drunken man wandered into my corner. His look scared me. The man made suggestive gestures that scared me even more. I wanted to move away but returned to my place, knowing that Maryla depended on my signals.

Luckily, he couldn't keep his balance and fell on the ground when two running men passed him in a hurry. I guessed that the sudden headlong rush of people trying to leave the marketplace signaled an entrance of NKVD, and so I hid the bag and warned Maryla. Then we ran together holding hands.

In step with this new life, I was learning fast. I knew where to go in case of danger and where to meet Maryla if we lost each other. Usually this arrangement worked for us, but sometimes I couldn't find Maryla in the crowd.

On one occasion, while I sat on Maryla's brown bag watching the market, I saw the NKVD leading a man away. I hid the bag but then couldn't find Maryla. I felt lost in the crowd of strangers whose heads drifted high above my own head. I didn't know any of those faces. I walked around in confused circles but couldn't find Maryla. I came up to a chestnut tree and stared at its last dangling leaves. Finally, I climbed that tree and looked down. In a stir of moving, drifting, oscillating heads I saw the red disk of Maryla's beret.

Lwow was a thriving city. I didn't thrive. I walked slowly with my head down. I was perpetually cold. I shivered in Maryla's old sweater. My nose was running all the time.

"Znowu masz katar" (your nose is running again), said Maryla. My sniffles greatly annoyed her. When we came home Maryla threw a long reddish-brown fox fur toward me.

"Here, wear this."

I caught the fox by his stiff, stuffed head adorned with shiny black eyes made of glass.

"Put it around your neck, like so," said Maryla, turning down the fox's head. The fur touched my neck, like an open palm.

"That should keep you warm," said Maryla, spreading the fox paws over my chest. She pressed the clasp under the fox's chin and opened his mouth. The clasp bit on the furry paw.

"Before the war I wore this fox every day," she said dreamily. "I wore my silver fox only for special occasions." Maryla displayed the other fur, whose silvery-white hair contrasted with black like someone's graying head.

"Silver foxes are rare and very expensive," Maryla put the fur back into a narrow box.

The next day, wearing Maryla's fox to the market, I yielded to its soothing, tender touch. I felt warm, but I knew that I looked ridiculous when two men passed us on the street. One fixed his gaze on the fur collar and said laughingly, "*Stara malenka*" (a little old one). I was short and thin and walked fast to keep step with Maryla. The fox's tail traveled across my back like a furry overstuffed pendulum. Eager to remove the collar I pressed on the clasp under the fox's chin. The clasp pinched my finger as if the fox wanted to bite me. Two glassy black eyes looked at me scornfully.

Tall, alert, chain smoking, Maryla moved quickly: right hand in her breeches pocket, a lighted cigarette in the left. The peddlers helped each other, and Maryla seemed happy among them. Lighting a cigarette from each other, they'd send a signal with a turn of an eye. I watched smugglers bending over her shoulders, blowing air at her neck. They drank vodka and sang their own version of *carpe diem*.

Return to Lwow

Hej uzyjmy zywota
Bo zyjem tylko raz.

Let's enjoy life to the full
Since only once we live.

All around me people rushed, moving about, selling, buying, solving, winning, losing, gaining. On a windy day I met Bronia. She stood with her hands pushed into the sleeves of her fur coat. She whispered something to Maryla, but the wind drew her voice and I couldn't hear what she said. Bronia held out her hand.

"Good morning," I said.

"Don't talk this way to an adult," Maryla corrected me promptly. "Say *caluje raczki*" (I kiss your hands).

Under Maryla's gaze, I took Bronia's hand as told. "Did you say *caluje raczki?*" asked Maryla. "I didn't hear, say it again."

"*Caluje raczki,*" I repeated louder, placing a kiss on Bronia's hand.

Bronia adjusted her hat and took my hand. Her palm was sweaty.

"Come, I'll show you what to do." She led me to a stone monument and told me to watch the entrance to the market from there. During the next month Maryla and Bronia traded together. Later they separated but kept in touch. I ran errands for both of them.

At first sight, with wind blowing at her hair, Bronia seemed delicate, almost fragile. Heavy eyelids made her appear to be dreaming. She had a short and narrow nose, light brown hair, plucked, arched eyebrows, and round, hazel eyes. She wore dark-red lipstick on her round, full lips, which

113

seemed to move all the time. *"Jeden, dwa, trzy,"* (one, two, three), she counted aloud. While counting she curled her mouth into a pucker, pushed her tongue against her cheeks, and smacked her lips. Sometimes she moved her jaws forward and back, keeping her mouth slightly open, as if she were thinking of nothing at all. No matter what was going on, Bronia always seemed unruffled.

She was often surrounded by men. I recall Bronia's first customer because I noticed that his breath smelled of vodka. He bent and blew air at her neck. Bronia clasped her hands behind her head and laughed heartily.

I didn't want to stay with Bronia; I wanted to be close to Maryla, but Maryla, grateful for Bronia's assistance, implored me to make myself useful.

I remember one Soviet soldier who clicked his tongue when Maryla walked past him in the market. His name was Sasza. He was shorter than Maryla, with a small, shaved head, small ears, and an upturned nose. Later, he danced with Maryla at her apartment.

"Turn around, *dziewuszka*," he called and laughed, and clapped his hands.

Maryla's gray flannel skirt swirled up, above Sasza's head, like an umbrella in a whirlwind. Sasza caught her left knee and jumped from one knee to another in a fast step called *prisiudy.*

"*Oh, harasho, harasho.* You dance so well!" he called, still holding Maryla's knee. Then he left Maryla romping round the room.

One Russian soldier taught me how to read Cyrillic characters, but Maryla stopped me at once.

"You don't need to learn Russian," she said, hearing my repetitions.

One evening, a Russian soldier played for Maryla a tuneful melody using three empty tea glasses. His name was Grisha. I watched him tune the glasses to musical scale after Maryla served tea. The tall water-filled glass, when struck with a teaspoon, produced a short high-pitched sound like a church bell during the High Mass.

"*Pozhausta dziewuszka,*" said Grisha. "Bring me water."

I filled a pitcher; Grisha poured water and struck the glasses again. The teaspoon, like a magic wand, hit the glasses one by one. Then, he put his ear close to the glass, varying the level of water, checking and rechecking the sound, until, one by one, three glasses chorded. Chink, chink, chinked the glasses.

"*Wolga, Wolga . . .*" Grisha's high tenor soared.

"*Wolga Wolgaaa . . .*" I followed, but Maryla didn't like my singing. "*Spiewasz jak mysz*" (you screech like a mouse), she said, and I took my book to the staircase.

Usually, when Maryla had company I was free to read. When we were alone I cleaned the kitchen and washed the dishes after supper. She didn't like it when I wasted time with books. But when she had a visitor, she washed the dishes, sending me away.

"Why don't you go and read your book, now. Remember to tell me how it ends."

Maryla's apartment was on the fourth floor. Below, between the second and the third floors, was a brighter lamp. I read a book borrowed from

Bronia—*Dzikuska* (The savage girl), subtitled *A Love Story*—written by a popular author of sentimental romances, Irena Zarzycka.

This place on the staircase worked for me. Nobody bothered me there, and I didn't pay attention to the passersby who dragged their feet up the stairs after a long day's work.

"What are you reading?" asked a tall, thin woman who lived next door to Maryla. I had met her before. Her name was Sabina. Sabina laughed when I curtsied and said, *"Caluje raczki."*

"She has to learn good manners," Maryla insisted.

"Those are silly affectations," replied Sabina, laughing again.

Now, Sabina stopped to see my book. I stood up for my quick curtsy, but Sabina stopped me. She wore a string of amber beads strung in a graduated pattern with the largest bead in the center. Her hair, only slightly darker than her beads, was combed away from her face.

Sabina looked straight into my eyes, which surprised me again. Maryla's large gray eyes rarely looked at me. She talked to me while doing something else. Now, Sabina's dark, narrow eyes sparkled for me.

"What is it you are reading?"

"Dzikuska," I said, but Sabina was already reading over my shoulder.

"Don't read trash." She held the worn-out volume comically at arm's length, as if her sparkling brown eyes would be contaminated by contact with such a novel. A moment later she brought from her apartment a book bound in faded brown linen. "Read this instead. This is a classic written by a Nobel Prize–winning Polish author, Henryk Sienkiewicz."

Sabina's book took me away from my corner of the staircase to the Suez Canal and to the Sahara desert. Stas, a boy of thirteen, and eight‑year‑old Nel escaped from their pursuers. I couldn't stop reading. I had to know what had happened to Nel. Then, I followed Stas and Nel to an empty baobab tree, where they hid at night. I cried when Stas brought Nel safely to her father.

"This is so beautiful," I told Sabina, who stopped again to talk with me on her way home from work.

"Henryk Sienkiewicz wrote beautiful books. He was awarded a Nobel Prize. Do you know about Nobel? No, I didn't think you did. Look for any of his books."

Sabina spread a linen towel across the top step and sat down.

"Sit," she said, seeing me curtsy again.

"And stop that nonsense of kissing hands, at least when we are alone."

I sat. Sabina put a pile of books by her right hip. Sabina was slim; her yellow towel protected her skirt. She could see that my old, patched, woolen skirt didn't need protection, but she shared her towel with me anyway. She sat close to me and told me about Sienkiewicz. Her hair, tied behind her neck, brushed my cheek when she moved to get another book.

Until I met Sabina, I simply read any book that I could get; Sabina taught me to select. Later she gave me a small collection of poetry titled *Ballady I Romanse* (Ballads and romances).

TRAINS

"I think you will like this poet, Adam Mickiewicz," she said, spreading a green bordered towel on the stair to protect her skirt.

"Read it aloud," she suggested, and when I finished she challenged me again:

"You read well; could you repeat any of this?"

Without looking at the page, I repeated for Sabina:

> ona mu z kosza daje maliny
> a on jej kwiatki do wianka
> pewnie kochankiem jest tej dziewczyny
> pewnie to jego kochanka

> she gives him berries from her basket
> he gives her flowers for her wreath
> he must be her beloved
> she must be his

"Good. You have a good memory. Do you know any other poems?" she asked.

"Yes," I said and recited "Locomotive" for her.

"Would you like to borrow that book?"

"Oh, yes," I said with so much enthusiasm that Sabina added quickly:

"This volume comes from my set of Adam Mickiewicz's collected poems. I can't give it to you, but you can keep this book of Mickiewicz's poems," she said, placing on my palm a small volume titled *Selected Poems by Adam Mickiewicz.*

The book opened on a dried nasturtium. Once bright and yellow, now it was pressed into a flat, almost translucent reminder of someone else's past. *What did it mean to Sabina?* I wondered, plotting a story about a girl meeting a boy in a staircase.

From now on, when I had time, I read poems from my own book, the only object that was my own since I parted with my family. I memorized many poems by this great Polish romantic poet, Adam Mickiewicz. I thought that I would never part with Sabina's gift, but when we departed from Lwow, two months later, I was forced to leave the book behind in an empty apartment. There was no room for books in our luggage.

During that time in Lwow I found that I was good at games. Witek, the janitor, played checkers with me and let me win sometimes. Having tasted victory once, I played better next time.

In like manner I got my first taste of arithmetic from Witek.

"Can you figure that?" he'd ask, looking at Maryla's bottles ready for the market. "She paid me ten rubles for one liter of *spiritus*, which I bought for seven rubles. How much did I earn?"

The next evening he challenged me with another problem. Then, one evening he gave me a multiplication table that I memorized during the next weeks.

"How much is five times eight?" he'd ask me, winking.

One evening Witek opened Maryla's round 100-count box of cigarettes, named *Mewy* (The seagulls).

"How long would this box of *Mewy* last if Maryla smoked only twenty cigarettes each day?" He winked at me knowingly. We both knew that Maryla chain smoked all the time. They were both heavy smokers; late at night smoke drew magic lines over their heads.

Later in Lwow, Maryla smoked *Sporty* again. Even the word *Sport* holds for me reminders of past discomfort. I remember the box with large blue letters, *Sporty*, and a silhouette of a disk thrower, and the twitch at the corner of Maryla's mouth when I handed her a last box with only three cigarettes. She could ignore hunger, but she was unable to live without smoking. I often tried to hide a few cigarettes for Maryla. I'd envision a moment when I'd produce a hidden cigarette for Maryla and she'd thank me heartily. But sometimes I couldn't find them afterward.

I remember one night when Maryla had nothing to smoke. I had a bad dream that night. I dreamed that I was up to my hips in deep snow. I heard someone calling me to come back, but I didn't stop walking, pushing through the snow, sliding back, disoriented. Then, I heard a rumbling sound like an avalanche and started to run in a chaotic effort to escape. Harsh sound woke me in the middle of the night. Half asleep, I saw Maryla roaming around the apartment like a tiger in a cage.

"I don't have anything to smoke," she said angrily.

I had hidden four cigarettes somewhere, but now, awakened from a nightmare in the middle of the night, I couldn't remember where I put them. For some minutes I looked in the drawers, but I couldn't find them. Maryla waited, moving her lips in a sucking motion, while I fumbled, searching box after box without success. I even looked under Maryla's silver fox—nothing.

Maryla walked round the room. She couldn't be still. Trying to help her, I went outside to look for some cigarette butts on the street. I brought them home to Maryla, who rolled from that a cigarette for herself in a scrap of newspaper. She was happy now.

Some weeks before, when I went for the first time to buy cigarettes for Maryla, I couldn't find my way back. Unsure of which way to go, luckily I noticed the red canna blooming. But I returned empty handed.

That particular evening, not having anything to smoke, Maryla put some leaves of dried salvia, which she kept in her kitchen cabinet as a cure for stomachache, into a thin tissue paper and rolled a cigarette. When a violent cough forced her to extinguish that cigarette as soon as she inhaled, she pushed the butt so hard that the rounded bottom of her glass ashtray slid on the polished wood, spilling the ashes over her dining room table.

———

Late that fall, Maryla met Rysiu, a local pastry maker. I knew at once how much Rysiu despised me. One day Maryla showed him the photograph of my first communion. Rysiu glanced at the photo, then quickly pushed it away. His expression hardened. He wasn't fooled. He could tell that I was a Jewess. He didn't like it. Soon after moving in with Maryla, Rysiu was mobilized and left Lwow with the Polish army. As a trained pastry maker, he knew how to cook, which proved useful. He wasn't sent to the front line and found a safe place in the kitchen in Lublin. Soon he was placed in the Polish officer's club as a cook and wrote to Maryla to join him in Lublin. In December, on Rysiu's advice, Maryla also joined the army and left Lwow.

Before we left, Maryla's neighbors shared news about the future of Lwow and endlessly discussed the news: hearsay, gossip, news heard on the radio, any news. I listened to their endless deliberations. The fate of Lwow was at the center of every discussion. One evening someone heard on the radio that Churchill gave Lwow to the Soviets.

The thought of leaving her apartment distressed Maryla. She hesitated, postponing her departure. Through the following days and weeks, right until late November of 1944, Maryla alternated between wanting to stay in Lwow and getting ready to leave at once. For a while the rumors had it that Lwow would be spared.

Then the uncertainty ended. Lwow would be a part of the Soviet Union. Witek brought a newspaper to Maryla's apartment and said to leave as soon as possible. He watched as Maryla rolled a cigarette, lit it, and said that she would stay. She still didn't want to leave her apartment.

A letter from Rysiu set things in motion. He had a place for her in Lublin. Early one morning, December 1, Maryla went to the military office and enlisted in the army. She returned late in the afternoon and began packing her belongings into a large forest green duffel bag. "We left Lwow on St. Nicholas Day," Maryla always said, recalling our departure, on December 6, 1944.

Lublin

And then I was in Lublin. In late 1944 Warsaw was still occupied by Germans, and Lublin was the temporary Polish capital. The war was almost over, Lublin was free and I was free, but I still couldn't go to school. The army placed us in someone's apartment. Irma, the owners' daughter, went to school every morning.

We lived in a small room with a table and a sofa. Maryla and Rysiu slept on a sofa; two chairs tied together served as my bed. Near at hand were books in a glass book-case, which stood by the wall, between two windows facing the street. I could browse through the books and read what I wanted.

"You can read any book you like," said Irma's father, unlocking the door. "When I was a boy I liked this one," he said, removing Sienkiewicz's *Potop* (Deluge), from a shelf above my head.

I remember Irma's father fondly; a short, bearded, bespectacled man who opened his bookcase and let me read his books.

"Why aren't you in school?" he asked one day, seeing me sitting by the window. "Your mother should enroll you in Irma's school. You could walk to school with Irma."

TRAINS

That evening, I asked Maryla to let me go to school.

"I didn't go to school when I was your age," said Rysiu, who overheard my plea. "I had to work for a baker scrubbing pots every night. He hit me on my head; that's why I can't learn as fast as you."

I sat at the window of the apartment looking at normal life; normal, despite the war. I watched girls returning from school: dark pinafores, book packs. I wanted to go to school and was envious of Irma. Irma, also eleven, wanting to sleep longer, leaving home in the morning; grinning provocatively, sourly. Irma coming back from school in her neat uniform.

For a while it seemed that the war would be over very soon. Rysiu dreamed of opening a pastry shop after the war. He would need me in his store. Now, in Lublin, Rysiu worked as a cook in the officers' club, content to stay out of the battlefield. Maryla also worked in that kitchen. They both wore the Polish army uniforms and soft, four-cornered hats called *rogatywki*.

Alone in the crowded streets, I watched girls my own age going to school as if nothing had happened. Later in the day, I watched them on their way home. I dreamed of being one of them, in school. Alone, lost in the crowd, I watched them go by. Nobody seemed to notice that a school-age girl was on the street during school hours.

When the streetlamps lit up I headed back to the officer's club to be there in time for the show. I remembered going to the theater before the war. One play about a wolf and Red Riding Hood stands out in my memory now. The actor playing the wolf had a deep voice.

The officers' club in Lublin, called *Centralny Dom Zolnierza*, was located on a busy street, or so it seemed to me then, in December of 1944. The building seemed large. To enter, I had to approach a tall gate where two soldiers stood checking everyone's identity. Despite my civilian clothes, I could enter at any time. In the daytime, I went straight to the kitchen; at night, I ran upstairs to watch the show.

Before taking their show to the front, actors rehearsed and performed in the officers' club. I saw three productions during my stay in Lublin. First was a satirical review, *From Morning till Night,* that gently ridiculed the typical routines of a soldier's day. Next was a musical comedy: *The Queen of the Neighborhood.* The actress came to rehearsals still wearing a soldier's uniform. She disappeared into her dressing room and came to the stage dressed as a peasant girl. She was protected by a pair of petty thieves, Antek and Kantek, who were always ready to rescue her. Then came *Wesele* (The Wedding), by a great Polish poet, Stanislaw Wyspianski. From my seat high on the balcony I saw *chochol*, a rosebush wrapped for winter in withered straw, who came to the wedding from a garden patch. I watched him dance in the circle of light.

After the show I ran back to the kitchen, where Maryla was swapping jokes with the soldiers. I walked back from the theater behind Rysiu and Maryla. In the night the scene grew in my imagination; more real than the strange turns of my own life. I felt wind dashing through my coat and heard a name whispered to the wind. I lay wide-awake, remembering.

Some days I stayed in the officers' club the whole day waiting for the show. One day I wandered onto the empty stage, where a trunk full of props lay open. I touched the sword and felt empowered like a brave knight from Sienkiewicz's *Potop.*

On that night, walking behind Rysiu and Maryla, I prayed for courage. When Rysiu stopped to greet a passerby I asked Maryla again to enroll me in school. But she turned me down.

I was baptized in December 1944, in Lublin. One day, as soon as Maryla and Rysiu went to work, I walked into a church. It was Wednesday morning and the church was empty, except for a sexton putting fresh candles into the candelabra in front of the altar. When the priest came and sat in his seat, I told him that I wanted to be baptized. He rose from his seat, looked at me, walked me slowly to the vestry, and without any delay performed the rite. That was all.

A Train Missed

On January 17, 1945, Warsaw was liberated from the Germans, and soon we were on the road again. Another departure and another arrival, not by train this time, but on an open army truck full of soldiers. As the trucks rolled toward Warsaw, I sat in the corner on one side, Maryla with Rysiu on another. In the twilight the trees along the highway grew darker. We drove till midnight, stopped at somebody's house to get a few hours of sleep on a floor in a crowded room, and then continued until we reached Warsaw.

The city was in ruins. Our cavalcade of open trucks rolled slowly through streets covered with broken bricks and with the debris of fighting. I saw tears in soldiers' eyes; some were openly sobbing while our truck pressed onward amid the scattered remains of the once vibrant city now covered with broken relics of the previous life: lamps, metal wire, fixtures hanging, dangling in the wind. I leaned back in the truck, looking at residues of other people's livelihoods, snow covered oddments, metal scraps bent, rusted, sticking out from the concrete. On my left a lantern with a lamp missing. On my right, a store sign, *"UBRANIA MESKIE"* (Men's clothing), like the sign over my father's store in Lodz, before the war.

In the ruins some people were setting down their belongings, hanging blankets to replace missing walls. On a sidewalk, behind a makeshift oven formed from two parallel standing bricks, a woman was cooking her meal.

———

I still remembered this ride through ruined Warsaw when, years later, I recited a poem, "Ab Urbe Condita," in the Theater School in Lodz.

"Buy fresh pastries" (*do swiezego ciasta).* This ode to a stubborn street seller amid ruins of the destroyed capital of Poland was written by the same poet, a Polish Jew, Julian Tuwim, whose verse for children, "Locomotive," I once recited in the Warsaw Ghetto.

"Buy fresh pastries . . ."

———

Soon after that ride through the ruins of Warsaw, I was selling pastries and cookies on the streets of Pruszkow and on the electric train, EKD, that connected Warsaw with the surrounding towns: Grodzisk, Milanowek, Podkowa Lesna.

A storm is raging outside. I sit by the window in my home in Jackson, Michigan, recalling another stormy night fifty years ago and my lonely walk along the railroad tracks, in August 1945, when I was twelve years old.

We only passed through Warsaw and then moved further south-west to Tworki, near Pruszkow, where the Polish army took over part of a well-known mental hospital. I still couldn't go to school. I had a little stand formed from four bricks on which to rest my tray of pastries and cookies. Bricks were everywhere. A popular cartoon showed a robber holding a brick against the skull of a passerby. The caption said:
"Won't you buy a brick from me?"

TRAINS

———

In Tworki, Rysiu and Maryla worked in the officers' kitchen located behind a brick wall on the grounds of the hospital. We lived in a rented room outside the hospital. Rysiu and Maryla slept on a sofa; my bed was again formed from two chairs pulled together. Our landlady, Monika, was a kind gray-haired widow who couldn't understand why Rysiu treated me so badly. She supported herself by knitting sweaters for a local store and noted my knitting skills.

Coming back from the army kitchen Rysiu hid butter and sugar under his soldier's uniform. He called his loot *boki* (side stuff). At night, Rysiu baked pastries in Monika's kitchen, and I helped him with his chores. Then, he sent me off to sell his pastries on the street.

Rysiu's enterprise proved successful. The first day I sold the entire tray, and he whistled a cheerful polka while counting the money. After that Rysiu sent me every day. All he wanted was to own a pastry store after the war.

Rysiu set up a stand at the train stop, and I stood there selling pastries to the waiting passengers. There was an open train booth with a schedule on the wall and two wooden benches opposite each other. Sometimes, when the weather was bad, I sat under the tin roof of the booth. The rain outside would make people rush along without looking at a girl with a tray of pastry. I sat there for hours, watching the crowd, trying to sell. People rushed to work in the morning and rushed home afterward, while I sat there, waiting.

Rysiu wanted to earn money for his own pastry store. He counted the days till the war would be over. At night he counted the day's earnings. He made more pastries, which I sold on the street, or on the train, or at the train stop. Instead of going to school, I took my tray to the street calling, "*Ciastka, swieze ciastka!*" (pastries, fresh pastries).

On one rainy day an old man sitting across from me on the wooden bench said, "I will pay for two pieces of this torte if you will eat them instead of me." One single act of kindness came my way during those days. I declined. The old man boarded the train, and I didn't sell anything in the rain that afternoon.

On Sundays I sold ice cream during the soccer games at the stadium in Pruszkow. Disembarking from the tramway in front of the entrance to the soccer field, I was alone in the jubilant crowd. Families went to the games to be together; fathers and sons, sisters and brothers, mothers and daughters. I looked at them and felt abandoned and alone. Those were the last days of war, and large crowds went to the stadium every Sunday. I wandered among them, calling, *"Lody, lody, lody!"* (ice cream). I stood close in the mass of people, yet so far apart. I felt desolate, abandoned, and lost.

One day I walked back from the soccer field carrying unsold pastries on my tray. As I expected, Rysiu was furious.

"You cursed Jew!" he yelled. "Don't you know better than to come back before all the pastries are sold? Don't even try to bring any of this back. Next time I'll lock you out."

The end of the war was uneventful. Rysiu waited for his discharge from the army, and I sold his pastry on the street. Some days I would sell Rysiu's candies to the passengers on a train. Rysiu made chocolate candies late at night in Monika's kitchen, and when they hardened I wrapped them in brightly colored tinfoil. The next morning I packed them onto my tray, which I carried on two leather straps secured over my neck; this way I could maneuver my tray even in a crowded train. One day I almost lost my balance as the train veered toward the side, and I was relieved that my tray was still securely tied.

As earlier, in Lublin, I watched with cynical disdain as Maryla got ready to take Rysiu to his post when he had to keep guard at night. Here was a grown man in a soldier's uniform afraid of darkness. To spite Rysiu I trained myself in courage. The same girl who three years ago was so fearful of a goose was now fearless. Or tried to be.

On the night of the storm, before the last train left, I was selling candy at the train stop about five kilometers from Pruszkow. People walked along the road, and I walked with them trying to sell until it began to rain. At first I walked back slowly until the rain intensified. I was still away from the station when I realized that there weren't people around me anymore and the rain changed to a downpour. I hid under a tree to protect my tray. When the rain stopped I returned to the station but the last train had already gone.

I adjusted the straps on my tray, and started to walk back along the railroad track. Walking alone under the trees that stood on both sides of the track, I tried not to cry. When it started to rain, I hid under a tree; when the rain stopped, I continued walking. Later, the strong wind pulled out some trees and threw them across the railroad track. I tried to move around by taking advantage of the lightning flashes, but it was dark, and I lost my balance and landed in the mud. And then, it began to rain again, and again I hid under a tree. When the rain finally stopped I came home. Maryla and Rysiu didn't show any emotion when they saw me wet and tired, but this time Rysiu didn't say anything about the unsold candy.

And then came the end of the war, and Rysiu's discharge from the Polish army. Rysiu wanted a fresh start, and we moved westward to *Ziemie Odzyskane* (The recovered lands). That's what the Polish government called the western territories given to Poland after the Yalta Conference. Shortly before our departure Maryla bought a Saint Bernard puppy and named her Aza. I watched how Maryla hugged Aza when we took a train to Zabkowice.

Poniedziałek 9/IX - 1946 r.

Dzisiaj wróciłam ze szkoły w bardzo dobrym humorze. Mieliśmy dzisiaj właśnie pierwszą lekcję fizyki, którą bardzo lubię. Przytem pani, która nam tej lekcji udziela, bardzo mi się podoba. (Nie ze względu na jej powierzchowność, lecz na jej sposób ~~my~~ uczenia.) Wreszcie wszystko mię dzisiaj cieszy. Na pierwszej lekcji wybieraliśmy samorząd szkolny. Wysuwaliśmy kandydatury i potem głosowali. Z czterech kandydatów, ja otrzymałam

Zabkowice 1945–1948

In 1946, I began to keep a diary. Now, this diary brings back my years in Zabkowice. Today is Tuesday, June 8, 1993. I go into a storage area in our home in Jackson to search for a brown box marked "Diary and Notebooks." There, tucked away in the dark closet, behind boxes with old Polish books, I find my old diary and touch particles of my past adhering to the musty pages. The first entry, September, 1946.

One year earlier, in October of 1945, we arrived in Zabkowice, a small town in the Sudety region that was previously a part of Germany and now had been given to Poland. Rysiu, still wearing a soldier's uniform, went to the city hall and asked for an apartment. The city officials placed us in an apartment previously owned by a German family. The owners, a short, nervous, older woman and her tall, overweight daughter, still lived there. The women kept one room; Rysiu and Maryla took the larger bedroom; I slept in a study on a leather sofa. In the middle of a night a strange, metallic sound woke me up. I jumped up ready to run away, but it was only a grandfather clock in a corner across the room.

In the morning, unable to find the dog, Aza, I wandered into the kitchen. The German women looked at me, trying to guess what my search was about.

"Bowwow," I barked like a dog.

"Ah! *Der Hund!*" said the older woman raising up the tablecloth, and Aza emerged, wagging her tail. That was my first lesson in German. I soon learned more when Rysiu put me behind the counter of his pastry store. At first, many of my customers were Germans, and I learned to greet them and to count in German. Later, the Germans left Zabkowice.

Among the remains scattered on the floor of our apartment was a black ledger with only a couple of pages used. I tore those pages out. On the first clean page I wrote Sunday, September 8, 1946. Then I turned to the last page of the ledger and recorded there places where I had lived before. Although that list included some of my hiding places, I didn't mention my hiding experiences.

I didn't make any entry, not even a camouflaged one, about my Jewishness, nor about my real family. Maryla figures there as *Mamusia* (Mother), and Rysiu as *Tatus* (Father). After our parting in 1948 I put quotation marks around those words. In revenge or as editorial comment? Symbolic mutilation?

But that came later. Then, in 1946, I longed for Maryla's affection. I listened to the endearing ways she called her dog: *Aza, Azunia, Aziutka, Azenka,* Azka . . . I watched her cuddling stray animals and waited for a pat on my head. I made little gifts for her and waited for her touch.

It never came. Maryla needed my work, not my affection. I worked as hard as I could, but she was rarely satisfied.

Rysiu punished me for mistakes and pushed me to do more work. At first I helped upstairs where Rysiu made tortes for his store. Equipped with a large beater he stood for hours whipping eggs. Then, he put the batter into forms and baked them in the oven. Without any mechanical device Rysiu was able to whip a dozen eggs at a time with ease. "Just elbow grease," he would say. I was too small and too weak for this kind of work. Yet he forced me to do the heavy work that really required strength and skill.

Each day began for me with a laborious whipping of eggs. To make the buttercream for a torte, Rysiu would put twelve eggs and 1/4 kilo of sugar into a large copper bowl. I had to whip that mixture. Only later, when the cream turned to a light color, would Rysiu take over. Then, I would whip the second batch of cream while Rysiu was adding small chunks of butter to the first batch. When the cream had the consistency of a heavy pudding, Rysiu added vanilla, sampling the mixture until he was satisfied with its taste.

At the end, four bowls of buttercream flavored with cocoa, coffee, vanilla, and almonds were ready and waiting for Rysiu's finishing of the tortes. With a long knife Rysiu sliced each genoise into four thin circles. In the meantime, I made syrup by cooking orange peels in sugar and water. Before assembling the tortes Rysiu mixed this syrup with rum, adding some tea to adjust the taste. Then, he moistened each slice of genoise with the syrup and spread the buttercream. Finally, he sprinkled the sides of each torte with cake crumbs. He was very strong. He was able to hold a large assembled torte on his palm, using his left hand only to quickly attach the cake crumbs to its walls. Then, contentedly singing, he filled large pastry bags with cream and set out to decorate his tortes.

———

Saturday, October 19, 1946
Today in the morning we all took communion, so we didn't have any classes. I wanted to take communion again, on Sunday, but for no reason there were shouts and fighting at home, so I couldn't.

———

Rysiu wanted everything done to perfection. One morning, he found the pipes broken and the basement filled with water. I had to pump this out with a hand pump, standing for hours in the flooded basement. Again, I couldn't go to school.

Sunday, December 15, 1946
I didn't write lately because I didn't have any time.
Also, since I don't sleep in the attic anymore, I
didn't have any place to keep my diary. I left my
diary in the attic. That's another reason why I
didn't write for such a long time. I decided not to go
to any movie and to save the ticket money, so I
could buy a used bicycle. I don't know whether I'll
save enough to buy a bicycle, but I hope.

At the end of 1946 Rysiu accepted two apprentices
to help him in the bakery, and sent me to work in
his store. Too small to be visible standing behind
the counter, I had to be elevated on a wooden soda
crate. Rysiu was afraid to let a hired helper come
close to the cash register, and he knew that I
wouldn't steal his money. So, I had to be in the
store all the time, even on Sundays. Today, I blame
myself for staying with them so long, but I didn't
feel free to go.

One thing I insisted on, was that I would go
to school. Since Maryla and Rysiu needed me at the

store, this demand caused frequent arguments. They let me know that going to school was a luxury. At first they didn't let me go to school, at all, but when I insisted, they finally agreed. I could enroll myself if I really wanted to.

I was born in 1933, but Maryla had registered my date of birth as 1937 and refused to correct it. In the fall of 1945 I went alone to the superintendent's office. Short, thin, with papers stating that I was only eight years old, I demanded to be placed in the sixth grade. They looked at me with irony and inquired why somebody more mature hadn't come to enroll me, but they sent me to a class anyway.

When I went to school I mingled with the students and thought that I was like them, but I wasn't. Being around others my own age was strange. My peers looked at me as a freak. Next year, already thirteen years old, I kept saying that I was nine. When I was acting my own age, other people thought my actions inappropriate for somebody so young when, in reality, I was already thirteen years old.

———

Wednesday, December 18, 1946
Yesterday we had visitation in school. They remained in my class during the lessons of History and of the Polish language. All went very well, but I

have a very serious problem because of my age. Pan Visitator (inspector) said that I wouldn't be able to stay in the seventh grade any longer. Maybe mamusia will go to school to talk to them. Today, mamusia went with tatus to Klodzko, maybe tomorrow they will be back.

Along with my falsified age, my work in the store separated me from my peers. I couldn't play with them. Rysiu opened the store early and closed it past midnight. Early in the morning I stood behind the counter until he came down to let me go to school. No time for homework; the store was always open, always busy. I did my homework in school, during class recess, when other kids played.

Saturday, December 21, 1946
Mamusia is back. Today is the last day of school before the holiday. I couldn't go to school because I had to work in the store. Yesterday I gave my

notebook to Pan Tymburski (my teacher). Today, he wanted to give it back to me but couldn't, since I wasn't in school.

———

I spent three unhappy years in Zabkowice. I can still sense this unhappiness when I read from the pages of my diary. Rysiu expected me to be grateful, but I often responded with a sneer to his angry curses. He believed that reading was a waste of time. "She reads books," he complained loudly. "I didn't have time to read; I had to work!"

They kept me captive in the store. Rysiu was hot tempered, ready to strike at the slightest cause, and Maryla always took his side. Anything would fuel his anger. Ten Cholerny Zyd!" (that cursed Jew), he often called me in his rage. "I'll kill you like a dog!"

Rysiu usually paid deep respect to his customers, and yet, he didn't hesitate to beat me in their presence. "The devil take you, you cursed Jew!" he cried out through an open window. "I'll kill you like a dog!" Somebody who heard Rysiu's angry curses must have repeated them to somebody else because one day two strangers paid us a visit.

They were looking for Jewish war orphans and came to collect me, but Maryla didn't let me go.

"After everything that I did for you," Maryla said to me, "You will betray me like Christ-killers betrayed Jesus Christ." She held my hand and whispered, "Don't go with them," and I obeyed.

I still can't forgive myself. I chose staying with strangers instead of joining my own people. Had I gone, everything would have been different for me. Maybe I would have traveled to Israel with those two Jewish scouts. At least I would have grown up in a Jewish orphanage. But under pressure from Maryla I refused to go with them. "After everything that I did for you," Maryla said to me.

Once I had a chance for a normal life, but I made the wrong move. I still blame myself for what I said then. "Now you are going to betray me like the Jews who betrayed Jesus," Maryla whispered to me on the dark stairway, and I said, "No."

Maryla and Rysiu needed me in the store and refused to let me go. I didn't want to leave without their permission, so I stayed. Only later, after Rysiu's sister came to work for him, did he finally agree to my departure. "Why won't you let me go?" I asked. At first they wouldn't hear of it, but then, one day, they said, "Yes." I went upstairs and gathered my belongings. Then, I went to a nearby garage and sold my bicycle for 1600 zloty, which enabled me to buy a one-way bus ticket to Wroclaw.

With Rysiu, Maryla, and their son
Zabkowice, 1947

Freedom

And then I was free. I felt it from the moment I got out of the bus. When I left Rysiu I found work in a store in the nearby city of Wroclaw and worked there until the end of the summer. But I wanted to get farther away from Zabkowice. I set my mind on Szczecin, a seaport in the northwestern part of Poland about 360 kilometers north from the area where I had lived with Rysiu and Maryla. When the summer ended, with my earnings, I bought a suitcase, a set of notebooks, and a one-way train ticket to Szczecin.

My train left Wroclaw in the evening. Alone, in a crowded compartment, I had the whole night for myself. I thought about my new life, trying to imagine what I would do, where I would live. I thought about my new school. But I didn't stop to think about my true identity. On that crucial all-night train ride I didn't return to my past, even in my thoughts. I was already fifteen years old. What happened to my brain? Where was my heart? Why didn't I stop and reflect?

TRAINS

My train stopped in the morning at the station in Szczecin. I checked my suitcase at the temporary storage in the train terminal, took a tramway leading to town, and strolled toward the tall building marked "School."

"Your papers, please," said a gray-haired woman in the school superintendent's office when I came to enroll. Accepting my transcripts, she added that it wouldn't be easy to maintain my four-point average in Szczecin. "Where do you live?"

"First school, then a job, then a place to live. I want to get into a good school before it is too late."

"Do you have family here?"

"No, I don't have any family."

She picked up the phone. "Hello, this is Mrs. Palka from the superintendent's office," she said to somebody on the other end. I listened. With her every sentence my life was taking a new turn. "Mr. Berent will come soon to fetch you," she told me. "Wait here until he comes. He is a nice man. His brother was the famous writer, Waclaw Berent. Did you read any of his books?"

"Yes, I did!" I had read Berent's *Silent Stones* in Lublin. It was one of the books in Irma's father's bookcase. "I will meet his brother?"

"We are trying to find a place for you in the orphanage, but you'll have to wait for an opening in a transit center."

Mr. Berent and his wife kept me in their apartment until there was room for me in the transit center. Then, from September 1948 until my high school graduation in June 1951, I lived in an orphanage called *Panstwowy Dom Mlodziezy* or *PDM* (State Youth House), first in Koszalin and later in Szczecin.

Freedom

To enroll I used my transcript from the
school in Zabkowice. Eager to get back my true age
I corrected my birth date from September 1937 to
June 2, 1933. "I am fifteen years old," I said loudly.
Correcting my birth date emancipated me. Another
small step would have taken me back to my true
self. But I didn't take that step. Still fearful, I
didn't tell anyone that my name was Miriam
Winter. I kept my false last name Dudek and
remained hidden behind my Christian name,
Maria, with its diminutive, Marysia.

I arrived in Koszalin just before school
started, in late summer of 1948. We lived in four
houses. In the middle one were our kitchen, dining
hall, and *swietlica* (activity room). The boys lived in
two other houses. Ours, the smallest, stood near the
orchard. Looking at that house I couldn't believe my
good luck. We lived like a large family and loved
each other.

Assigned to my room, I met my roommate,
Halina, a blonde and pretty girl, a bit shorter than
I. Danka, my other roommate, was still away. Our
room had white walls with light-yellow borders.
Three beds lined the walls. A guitar hung on a wall
above Halina's bed. Halina smiled often, liked
people, liked to be liked.

She never seemed tired. "We will wash our
window every Saturday," she decided as soon as we
moved in. In the morning I wanted to sleep, but
Halina, full of energy, brought a broom, and we
cleaned our bedroom. She took down the old, ink-
splashed curtains and sudsed them in soapy water
in a white enamel washbowl. Halina was neat.
While other girls' bedrooms occasionally would be

scattered with shoes, socks, and notebooks, Halina insisted that we keep our room in order.

She liked everything to be in place. She always hung up her school uniform and taught me to do the same. Her books were stored away in a box under her bed. Her mother's photograph hung framed on a wall. Everything had its place in our room thanks to Halina.

Every Saturday we polished our pine-board floor with old pieces of wool. Halina spread a reddish paste on the floor, and then the three of us stepped on rags, walking around until the floor shone the way Halina wanted. "It looks good now," she'd say, surveying the bedroom.

We wore dark-navy woolen uniforms, adorned with starched white cotton collars that Halina made for the three of us from an old pillowcase. She made starch from flour boiled to a mushy paste. She taught me how to iron. To keep our pleated skirts crisp, we arranged them for the night under our bedsheets, on top of the mattress.

Danka, a student in a vocational school, was almost as neat as Halina. She wore eyeglasses and had a small nose, pouting mouth, narrow low forehead, and shoulder-length blond hair that she set in paper curlers every night. She let me use her stenography textbook, and I taught myself how to use and read some of the shorthand signs.

Some evenings girls gathered in our room. Halina sang and played the guitar; I read and recited poetry. I admired Halina; she loved people, trusted them, felt safe even among strangers. Halina had an expressive face; she often furrowed her forehead, raising her eyebrows to make her point. She had a warm alto voice and liked to sing.

When she sang she bared her short, strong teeth. We called her *Squirrel*.

Those were good-hearted days free of anger and violence. In the fall we gathered apples from the old trees. When we cut classes we played cards in the orchard. We borrowed each other's blouses, skirts, shoes. We lived like brothers and sisters, with perhaps less fighting than real siblings. We formed close friendships, which we later continued. We dearly loved each other, but I was nicknamed *Pchelka* (a little flea) for my acerbic tongue.

Halina gave as much attention to her schoolwork as she did to our room. She was a good student, but not excellent, more diligent than bright. Although we went to different classes, we competed in school. I was a better writer, but Halina, who had perfect pitch, beat me in languages. She excelled in Latin and was a good athlete. I was faster in math.

Every morning we had breakfast in the dining room together. We ate rolls with jam and drank hickory coffee with milk. When we had dining room duties, we went around the room with a large wicker basket full of rolls.

After breakfast we gathered our books and got ready for school. Our orphanage was located on the outskirts of town. We usually waited for the rest of our group on a small volleyball court outside the boys' building. Then, we walked together, a three-kilometer stretch, talking, laughing, singing.

After school, we took turns in the kitchen and in the dining room. We spent our free time in *swietlica*, where we played games during the daytime and danced at night. The boys taught me to play ping-pong.

TRAINS

Outside we played volleyball. When I came to live in the youth house, I didn't know how to catch a ball. The boys taught me how to volley. Too short to spike, I learned how to serve, to ground a ball, and to cooperate on the field. Later, when we came to Szczecin, I could set up a good spike.

One winter's day we cut classes and went skating. I didn't want to cut classes; although Halina, my roommate, was graceful on the ice, I didn't know how to skate. This was the first year that I was finally free from working for Rysiu in his store. I liked school; I was competing for the first place in math, and I didn't want to go. But Leszek, Halina's admirer, brought two pairs of skates to our room and persuaded me to join them. So, while other kids from our orphanage went to school, four girls and eight boys skated on the lake.

The road turned uphill, and my feet began to ache. Clumsily I tried to move my legs. I didn't have a chance to fall down; somebody was always close to hold me. I didn't feel clumsy; we held hands, sliding.

My cheeks tingled when we skated downhill coming back. Not a car on the road; nobody was there but us. We held hands across the road from shoulder to shoulder. We felt alone in the vast whiteness. Not lonely, alone. As we skated downhill, wind turned up our pleated navy blue skirts, showing heavy flannel drawers underneath.

We thought we were alone, but our counselor, Czeslaw, saw us there. When we noticed him, cross-country skiing along the field, we expected trouble. He was soft spoken and inspiring, but also demanding. Light haired, tall, and thin, he looked even thinner in his black turtleneck. We didn't know then that he had tuberculosis.

Halina had street smarts enough for the two of us. "Maryska, we better clean our room well." We dusted and cleaned the floor. We even polished the ceramic tiles of our heating stove that stood in the corner. We worked the whole afternoon trying to redeem ourselves.

When evening came Czeslaw entered our room as Halina had predicted. Raised on his tiptoes in search of overlooked dust, he ran his finger along the carving high on the top of the wooden door and showed us how much gray dust he had uncovered. But he didn't report us. Years later, when we became friends, Czeslaw laughed, recalling those pleated skirts and pink flannel drawers. Today, Czeslaw has lung cancer; when I call him across the ocean we laugh together.

Evenings we danced. In the corner of *swietlica* stood an old piano, and Witek, who knew how to play, was the most popular boy.

"Witek, play," we would ask as soon as he'd enter the room. He always obliged. Zosia, Witek's girlfriend, usually sat by the piano while he played.

At first, a new girl in the orphanage, I didn't dance with boys, but Halina taught me some steps and danced with me. Halina, strong, limber, and graceful, danced well. It took many lessons before I gathered the courage to waltz with a boy. When a boy named Mietek asked me to dance I turned red, but, too shy to refuse, I dragged my feet heavily.

I liked to watch how other girls danced. My roommate Danka always danced with Tomek, who held her thin waistline with large hands. Danka's skirt swirled round her hips when she waltzed;

turned up lips made her appear to be smiling. Olek, who played ping-pong with me, danced with Krysia, a slender girl with large green eyes and robust red hair. When Krysia waltzed I couldn't look at anybody else.

Our director danced, carrying his daughter Lilka, on his shoulders. He was a kind and gentle man, and children adored him. His large round face reminded me of Grisha, who used to dance in Maryla's apartment in Lwow. Tall and sturdy, the director liked to dance and kept us circling together. He called out arches, squares, chains, and serpentine twists. Lilka, thin and short turned under his arms. "*Odbijany*," he would call in his booming voice, which was a signal to change partners.

Shortly before ten o'clock one of the girls would start dancing with our director to coax him to postpone the closing time. Pretending that he didn't notice he'd burst forth, galloping across the room in a *Krakowiak*, a Polish national dance.

On warm summer nights we danced outside. None of us had radios, but one boy, Staszek, had a harmonica and we danced on the sidewalk or wherever we heard music.

I went to ninth grade in Koszalin in 1948. At the same time Romek, my future husband, also a ninth grader, danced in another youth house in Karpacz in the southwestern part of Poland. Romek came from a different background: a Pole, not a Jew, he didn't have to hide; his siblings and his mother still lived in the same village where the war had met them in 1939. Yet, Romek's days in the youth house turned to a beat similar to mine and formed him in a mold not unlike mine.

Freedom

"You have the same mannerisms," remarked Czeslaw shortly after I met Romek fourteen years later, in 1962. We waltzed with the same zeal when we met. We still do.

———

Transferred to Szczecin in the summer of 1949, I lived again with Halina in a larger youth house, which I left in 1951 after my high school graduation.

Łódź - Ozorków - Toruń; - Rokha - Wiśniowa Góra - Tuszyn Las - Ożarów -
wa - Ozorów - Skarżysko - Świów - Grudec, - Tarnów - Rzeszów -
Głogów-Lublin - Włochy - Warszawa - Pruszków - Ząbkowice -
Włodzko - Gdynia - Gdańsk - Inowrocław-Wrocław - Szczecin -
Koszalin. - Goroki - K - Wilcza Góra - K - Słupsk - K - Szczecin,
K - Wambierzyce - K - Kłodzko - Polanica - Łązek - Radków.
- Raszewo - Mejszowina - W - K - Szczecin, - Trzebież -
Warszawa - Koszalin. - Szczecin - Koszalin - Skorzewa -
Bartoszewo - 5-cia - Świnoujście - Łobez - Skorzewo
Skorzewo - 6-cia - W-wa - Pruszków - Szczecin
W-wa - 5-cia - Gdynia - W-wa - 5-cia - Bydgoszcz -
- Pomorska Ogrzelżny - Bydgoszcz - 5-cia - Bydgo-
- Toruń - B - 5-cia - B-Kłośpurzakłów-B-z-Solecie-Bio-B-w-wa

Szczecin 1949–1951

I sit in my warm room in Jackson, Michigan. Romek, my husband of thirty-two years, goes to the garden to feed the birds. The snow is still falling, but the morning is windless and calm. On Kibby Road, slowly, soundlessly, a few drivers brave the slippery highway, headlights on. But the Oakridge side is still unplowed and undisturbed. Not a car dares to violate the hilly narrow street by my eastern window. Where once was a sidewalk, and the driveway, and the opposite sidewalk, now only whiteness talks to the falling snow. Pensive, pure, intensely still. Undisturbed. No one on the road. Not even the joggers. Only snow.

Inside, tall houseplants grow into a hothouse jungle with a large hanging orchid cactus centered above the window like a huge spider. One flower, a pink star, stretches its petals toward the light, unreal, like the paper flowers I used to make during the war.

The opposite window looks down the slope—there, Kibby Road and the lagoons. Against the slope, raspberry canes are crocheted like golden brown lace on a white antique blouse. A clump of *Sedum* (Autumn Joy) collects snow on dark faded seed heads. Two tall brussels sprouts plants are almost completely covered. Like a pair of tired walkers, they support each other against the freezing wind. One shorter, one taller, heads stretched forward, their knees bend to take another step.

Below, six wooden whiskey barrels, under trees salted by patches of snow, overflow with whiteness. The snow falls slowly, effortlessly filling gaps between the red cabbage leaves, turning two kale plants into a pair of pensive hoboes ready to climb the fence and run onto the frozen lagoon where, in the afternoon, Romek will skate circles on the ice.

Watching Romek lacing his black skating boots, I recall Koszalin's snowy landscape on the morning when I went skating on the lake with Halina. Then, as I visualize one tall spruce behind my bedroom window in Koszalin of 1948, wrapped in a snowy stillness like that of today, the smells and sounds of Koszalin merge into Szczecin, where I moved in 1949.

Looking back at my years in the orphanage I notice the interlacing of my life and Romek's. Like me, Romek moved from one youth house to another. When I skated in Koszalin, Romek turned circles on the ice in Zakopane. When I took a train to Szczecin, Romek moved to Karpacz. While I befriended Halina, he confided in Tomek. We traveled through different parts of post war Poland, yet our days in the Polish youth houses swayed to similar rhythms, so much so that when we met years later, in 1962, we both felt we knew each other. At times we had read the same authors and had emulated similar heroes.

Today is Tuesday, February 14, 1995. More than thirty years ago in Warsaw, Romek covered my feet with his coat while we waited for a bus on a wintry day. We wanted to visit Tomek, Romek's childhood friend. Romek had kept in touch with his best friend from the youth house, a boy met on his arrival when they were both thirteen. We asked Tomek to witness our wedding. Over thirty years ago, in the spring of 1963, I married Romek after he made me admit who I was. I had to marry him; he gave me back my real "me." In Lodz, in 1964, I gave birth to our first son. I wasn't afraid to give him a Jewish name: Daniel.

Later our world shifted again, tossing us across the globe. From Lodz in Poland, Romek, Daniel, and I traveled through Vienna and Rome to the United States, where David was born in 1970. We moved eight times through other places in Massachusetts, Pennsylvania, and Michigan before settling in Jackson. Jackson, a small midwestern town 200 miles east of Chicago, has kept me longer in one place than ever in my life. I have planted myself into the slope of my garden like the parsnips and cabbage and beets.

Inside, dry twigs of forsythia, forced in water in a tall crystal vase, yellow slowly. Seeing forsythia in bloom inevitably brings memories of Szczecin 1949–1951.

There, we lived in the outskirts of the city again, but now we rode a tramway to school. Otherwise, my life in the Szczecin's youth house, a larger youth house in a larger city, didn't differ much from that in Koszalin. Three girls in a narrow bedroom, three identical navy blue woolen uniforms, pleated skirts, long-sleeved tops, a white, hand-stitched collar on Halina's blouse. I lived with Halina and another girl named Hanka.

———

Again I went to a new school. Entering my classroom in an all-girls school in Szczecin, I brushed my cheek against the long brownish hair of a pensive girl. Her name was Krysia. Later we sat at the same desk. Another girl said, "Hi, my name is Baska. What's yours?"

"Marysia," I said. I still used that name, Marysia, although now I preferred it when friends called me by my nickname, *Pchelka*, (a little flea).

"I can hear the screech of Pani Szczerska's shoes," Baska shrieked and flew to her desk. She got up a minute later, leading me to a desk behind hers. "You may sit here. Magda isn't coming back."

Then, lowering her voice, Baska said:

"That was only a false alarm, but beware! You'll have to do something with your hair. Pani Szczerska won't allow curls in her school." Baska lowered her voice to a comic whisper: "Always wet your hair if you hear her screeching shoes."

People in Szczecin called us *Szczerytki*, a wordplay on the name of a strict monastery order—*Szarytki*—and on our strict principal's name, Pani Szczerska.

Soon I learned more from Baska. She liked to tell dangerous jokes in her girlish, high soprano, tenth grader voice. She was quick to laugh, perky, forward, self-assured, trusting, flirtatious, and free. In this guarded all-girl school, Baska's actions seemed even more forward.

A witty writer, Baska often read in class. Her essays had a sharp edge that I tried to emulate in my satirical column for the *Youth House Wall Gazette.* I soon discovered my friends laughing at my column. Exhilarated, I wrote more satirical stories in a similar manner. Earlier in Koszalin, I had already decided to be a journalist and had taught myself some shorthand from my roommate's handbook.

In the fall, I went to a nearby village with my classmates to help gather potatoes from the field. At night we made a bonfire and baked potatoes. Baska passed around a stone.

"When you get the stone, tell us about yourself, what you want, who you are . . . Pass the stone to the next girl if you don't want to talk."

The stone went from hand to hand, resting a while in the center of an open palm of the speaking girl. I watched and listened.

"I can't stand my parents," Baska said.

How can she say that? I thought.

Sitting around the fire, looking at those pampered, loved, protected girls, hearing anecdotes from their lives, I didn't want to reflect on my past. We didn't have anything in common. I passed the stone to Wanda, a short girl sitting on my right.

TRAINS

Back at my tall wooden desk, the second desk in the third row, I shared space with Krysia, the girl whose brown hair, now neatly braided, brushed my cheek on my first morning in this school.

"Tell me about your family," Krysia said.

"My father died shortly before the war," I lied.

"What did he do?"

"He worked in the post office in Lwow," I lied again.

"How about your mother?"

"My mother died of pneumonia during the war." I tried to sound natural, tough, sincere; careful not to reveal my Jewish identity. Later, I repeated the same lies when people asked about my past.

One day Krysia invited me to her home. Her grandmother sat by the window when we entered. Wind blew up the white lace curtains, shading her face like a veil, like snow. Krysia's mother, a graying, sturdy woman, a piano teacher, played Chopin's "Mazurka" on an old piano piled with sheets of music. Czerny's *Etudes* leaned against the lamp. Krysia's father sat at his desk.

Later, Krysia's mother called us to the kitchen, where we helped her make *kanapki*. Krysia spread butter on slices of bread, which we both garnished with cheese and chunks of marinated herring. Krysia's mother ladled soup into white porcelain bowls. We drank tea from tall, thin glasses and ate star-shaped sugar cookies called *gwiazdki* (little stars).

I felt a knot in my throat and wanted to cry when Krysia's mother lit a candle, but instead I bit into my cookie, crunching sugar between my teeth. In school I was jealous of Dorota, whose mother found her after the war. "Dorota's mother didn't stop searching until she found her. She loved her daughter so much," said my Latin teacher. My stomach turned. I felt sick. I thought I would throw up. I left the classroom and went home.

Back in my room I picked a quarrel with Halina. I was the only one who had nobody. I hid my eyes, which were too eager to cry. I was the only one without any relatives. There were no former neighbors, no parents' friends, nobody who had known me before or during the war. Even in the orphanage, the kids were not alone. Everyone had an uncle, or a father, or some distant family member. I had no one. If the whole family were wiped out, if no one survived, then I must be Jewish. So it didn't really matter that I didn't admit my identity. It mattered that I couldn't admit it.

There was a boy in our orphanage whose father came to reclaim him shortly after I arrived in Szczecin. His name was Wladek. Later, he lived nearby and visited us sometimes. On warm days he'd come to play volleyball, his manner altered, his face sweetened like Rysiu's pralines.

I picked a quarrel with Olek, who bragged about his large family. "I have plenty of cousins," he said, and I noticed how easily he moved, as if enclosed in a pink cloud. I wanted to move away when he stood next to me in line for our daily dose of *tran*, but I stopped and only closed my eyes.

TRAINS

Wiera shoveled a tablespoonful of *tran* into my opened mouth; I grabbed my bread and ran away.

We had *tran* every morning after breakfast. Disgusted when I got my first daily dose of this foul smelling whale oil—bad tasting but loaded with vitamins A and D and certainly good for us—I soon learned a few secrets from my friends:

"Swallow quickly; pretend you are eating an apple," said Halina.

"Bite into a chunk of bread with plenty of salt," said Janek.

When snow fell I knitted again. During my two years in Szczecin's youth house we received some packages of clothes sent from the United States by charitable organizations. From one packet I got a warm winter coat, from another, blue woolen trousers and a sweater too long for me. I pulled the wool from the sweater and knitted another that fitted me well. Later, from remnants, I made a vest in a bold Norwegian pattern. Afterward, with a girl named Renia, I knitted berets for sale.

Berets with large pompons in contrasting colors were in fashion in 1950, so Renia and I easily found a buyer for our products. Most stores belonged to the government, but we found one privately owned store. An older man sitting at the counter liked the beret and asked us to bring him more. We bought more wool and continued knitting and selling those berets.

Szczecin 1949-1951

Later I knitted in class. We sat in tall wooden desks, and I was confident no one would notice that while my eyes looked at the teacher my hands moved the knitting needles. Some days I'd read and knit at the same time.

"Show us what's under your desk," said my history teacher.

I gave him the book: *How the Steel Got Hardened,* by a Soviet writer, Nikolai Ostrovsky.

"I recommend this book to all of you," said the teacher, "but don't read during my lectures."

In the summer of 1949, before leaving Koszalin, I went to a scouting camp in Zambierzyce. Tall canes on a sandy strip of land by the Baltic sea. We set up the tents, stuffed mattresses with straw, built the latrines and the kitchen stove. There I started having doubts about religion. Our commandant, Zosia Wilska, held a campfire chat every night. Handsome and sincere, a biology teacher with soft brown eyes and brown shoulder length hair, she spoke softly and persuaded me that science has all the answers. She talked about evolution. I recall skits from that camp: two stones, hit one against the other; two sticks of dry wood spark, then fire, then match, then another girl looking civilized with neatly braided hair, flashlight against her face.

TRAINS

I believed Zosia. Back at the orphanage I read a book titled *Paganini's Damnation* describing the sufferings of young Paganini for which the Soviet author, Vinogradov, blamed the Catholic Church. Later, other books intensified those doubts until I became a nonbeliever. I read Polish translations of my favorite French authors like Anatol France, André Gide, Roger Martin Du Gard, and Romain Rolland and often copied excerpts from these books into my diary.

Yet, I still attended religion, a compulsory subject in our school then. I noticed how other girls treated nonbelievers and didn't want to be singled out.

We studied the history of the Catholic Church. I continued reading historical books, and those books brought my doubts into a sharper focus.

One morning I stumbled out of my bed and wrote in my diary, "I don't believe in God." Frightened, I tore the page out. At first I crumpled the paper and threw it into the wastebasket; then, afraid that someone might read my confession, I tore the page into tiny bits, which I burned in the white ceramic oven that stood in the corner of our room. But I didn't go to church anymore.

Bydgoszcz 1951–1953

In June of 1951 I turned eighteen and graduated from high school. All through that summer I worked for the state's department of education as a sort of human answering machine. I had a solitary job. After office hours someone would call from a summer camp. Most of the calls were just routine, and I dutifully recorded every one in an hourly ledger. I knew what to do in case of an emergency, but I didn't know what to do with myself. I had to leave the orphanage and felt cut off. Waiting for the calls I drew lines on scraps of paper, horizontal, vertical, diagonal, slanted, circles, looking for direction amid the tangled drawings.

Finally, I took a train to Bydgoszcz, some two hundred kilometers southeast, and enrolled in a school that trained instructors for amateur theaters. I didn't have to pay for my room and board in the dormitory run by the school; a scholarship covered my necessary expenses. But I felt lost.

On school trips we often went to Torun, a large city on the main Polish river, Wisla (Vistula).

TRAINS

I lived in Bydgoszcz, less than forty kilometers southwest from Torun, where I'd gone with my mother before the war. Just seven kilometers north from Torun was Lubicz; a small town by the river Drweca—my mother's birthplace, where I'd often played as a child. If I had wanted to, I could have walked from Torun to Lubicz in less than an hour. But I didn't go to Lubicz, and I don't know why.

For two years, from 1951 to 1953, I lived in Bydgoszcz in an old building close to the river Brad, in a narrow, long room with twelve other girls, and felt out of place. Unlike my friends from the orphanage, these girls had parents and a normal family life. I missed my friends, wrote long letters to them, and felt abandoned when they didn't reply at once.

All through that year, when my loneliness bent me down I went to the bank of the river Brda. Drifting about with no direction, not knowing what to do, I'd go to the river and watch it flow. I liked to sit near the edge, watching the waves go by. I felt like a sponge squeezed, left to dry, and then dropped into a puddle of mud.

I stood still during that entire school year. Like a stone thrown into a river I sank into my sadness. I wouldn't leave the riverbank when it rained. I felt the pelting on my skin, the water drenching my hair, trickling down my forehead, dropping on my eyelids. When the cold made me retreat, I'd run back to my dorm, where a warm shower masked my gloom.

Outwardly, I skipped and bounced. They still called me *Pchelka*. No one could come close to me; I aspired to be witty, acerbic, biting, and fast, yet still closely corseted, closed, cold, private. But sometimes my cover, like an eggshell too thin to transport, would crack in the theater, in the cinema, at night when no one watched me. I'd cringe hearing other's childhood recollections. I remembered the grinding feeling of lonesomeness when my roommate passed around a poppy seed cake saying:

"Mother baked *makowiec* for my visit."

I wanted to scream, but I ate the poppy cake and said nothing. Chewing, I smashed my envy into a smile.

I wore my mask in acting class and kept myself disguised. In the stagecraft class I learned how to make masks from papier-mâché. I made glue from flour mixed with cold water. I layered and pasted narrow strips of newspaper over a clean mold until, glued together; they followed the mold's shape. My mask fit well.

During the dance lessons we practiced the rounds, lifts, breaks, falls, slides until we knew them well; heels hitting the wooden floor, head up, body erect, back straight.

"Pull yourself up!" my teacher would yell if I'd slump.

"*Priamisa!*" called a visiting Russian teacher.

I learned how to choreograph a folk dance and later used that skill when I worked in Szczecin. I learned which steps belonged to a particular dance, how to create a sequence of those steps to show off the skills of the dancers.

I spent my days in a classroom or in my bedroom or on a stage. We performed almost every day in the factories in Bydgoszcz or in the neighboring townships.

Our director mounted a program for any occasion, weaving text and movement into a skillful montage. He would write in the morning, cast and rehearse in the afternoon, and send us off to perform at night. A good dramatist, he deftly mixed poetry and music with factory jargon. He contrasted an enrapturing dance with lyrical singing and alternated sad, tuneful, folk melodies with sharp, satirical, contemporary songs.

He cut poems to fit his thematic scheme: adapting the material to the town, to the factory, to the people, weaving connections, creating precise images. When he needed a scene fraught with danger he'd recall the war. To capture a feeling of doom he'd dramatize a scene from the war. He knew how to underscore any topic with the themes dictated by his superiors.

We had an enduring repertoire of choral singing and a set of folk dances that showed the skill of our boys and the beauty of the girls in vivid folk costumes.

Sometimes we'd start gliding in a *Polonaise*—one bending step and two straight steps—entering the stage slowly, stately, couple after couple in a solemn procession. Or, we'd leap forward in *krakowiak*, a merry skipping dance.

I learned to adapt to any size of stage; entering a large stage we'd fill the space with movement, gradually increasing the distance between each circling couple, spreading against the floor and the wings. Stooping, bending, winding, spiraling, sweeping, we'd extend over a large stage and fill each corner of a small one.

Marian, dark haired with burning black eyes danced with Krysia. I liked watching them dance, Krysia's loveliness made each dance beautiful. Her face, like that of a perfect porcelain doll, was close to Marian's face. Turning under his arm she'd steal one quick look and turn bashfully away.

Watching Krysia in *kujawiak*, a slow and melancholy Polish dance, I thought of a graceful reed from Oscar Wilde's tale about the "Happy Prince," which I had memorized in my high school English class.

Then we would dart out in *oberek*, a fast, vigorous three-qarter time dance. The boys had all the difficult poses and steps, while the girls just stomped around to support the boys' demonstration of athletic agility. I danced *oberek* with Staszek, not much taller than I and a fierce dancer and acrobat. In a turning wheel, Staszek, along with three other boys, would slide his feet into the center, while I'd pull him around like a shock of wheat after a harvest.

Once rain caught us in the middle of the performance while we danced on a podium outside, but people didn't move away. Some opened black umbrellas like dark mushrooms in the forest; others were drenched in the rain, watching.

After the show, we'd board the truck and sing under a starlit sky as we rode back to the dormitory. One night after the show, Marylka sang a simple lullaby about two kittens playing with a baby. Late at night the truck rattled on the stony old highway. Carol, thin, freckled, redheaded put his head on Marylka's shoulder, comically shutting his eyes. As if she wanted to lull a child, as if she didn't notice his clowning, Marylka sang:

TRAINS

aaa kotki dwa,
szare bure obydwa

two kittens gather
one as gray as the other

A moment before, sitting in the open truck, I sang with the others at the top of my lungs, but now stirred, I turned away from the lullaby.

Back in my narrow, long bedroom in the former attic, I'd write in my diary. Writing kept me sane. If it didn't help me master my feelings, at least it let me mask my distress. In winter I'd sit in a corner, with my back against the ceramic tiles of the *piec*—the heating stove, still warm—facing the narrow metal beds lined against the opposite wall where my roommates would set their hair on rollers made of strips of fabric fattened in the center with narrow cuts of newspaper.

On wintry mornings we took turns starting fires in this standard, white ceramic heating stove, almost six feet tall. One of these stood in a corner in most of the rooms in Poland.

"Do you know what's wrong with this *piec?*" Frania would ask innocently. Somehow, when Frania started the fire, the room would be blue with smoke. By evening the room would be blue again; most of the girls smoked.

"Oh, bed, there's nothing like a bed for a woman," Helena would whisper, leaning on her feather pillow. Curling her brown hair over thin newspaper strips Krysia would sigh comically, "I envy you for not having to put curlers into your hair." I often managed to scrawl a few words in my journal, but I didn't say that during the war children called me *Zydowa* because of my curly hair.

We'd talk loudly before going to sleep, then stop and listen to Frania. Frania, who couldn't start a fire in the *piec*, lighted any room with her voice. She had long brownish braids, large gray eyes, and an ear for poetry. Her strong jaw, jutted slightly forward, gave resonance to her words. On stage, while other girls wiggled, Frania listened intently.

We met for classes in a small room adjacent to the kitchen. The smell of cooking would seep into the room unexpectedly. A wooden wall with a serving window in the center separated us from the kitchen, but no wall could stop the cooking smells. Just before dinner, the tempting smell of cooked cabbage and of boiling potatoes would become unbearable. In the middle of the lecture all we could think about would be food. Sometimes one of us would knock at the serving window asking for bread. Often we'd ask the teacher to cut the class short. Then, we'd run to our bedroom to make *cogel-mogel*. We sat on our beds turning teaspoons in porcelain mugs. One egg yolk and three teaspoons of sugar in each mug. We stirred until the dark-yellow egg yolk turned lighter to a sweet almost white cream. My roommates got eggs and sugar from home and always shared the contents of a food package. I turned my teaspoon, squashing the flash of envy.

TRAINS

I started looking at passersby trying to guess who they were. Once coming back from the river I followed a couple on the sidewalk; they were of equal height—she blonde and slim, silent, he darker. Street lanterns stitched them together thigh by thigh; walking arm in arm they looked like one. I walked slowly behind them. A star cut through the dark sky, an airplane. The sound came closer, frightened me, made me think of war.

Earlier, shortly after my arrival in Bydgoszcz, a boy complained that he had seen a rat in his bedroom. His name was Jurek. I turned my head and stared at him while the teacher analyzed a play. Jurek curled his fingers over his cheeks. His clean, scrubbed, pink face looked shy while he watched the teacher with glinting eyes. Then he stood up:

"Last night I saw a rat running across my bedroom."

"Is that the conflict or the exposition?" asked Carol, and the group burst into laughter.

"I saw a rat," Jurek repeated in a tearful voice. "I won't stay here any longer."

The next morning he moved out. I laughed with my class, but I knew well enough that rats visited our old building close to the river Brda. Once Krysia's mother bought her a pair of brown, cork-wedged shoes, and the rats chewed up the cork.

Looking at Jurek's pink-scrubbed face I thought of Maryla and her dog Aza. In my mind's eye I could still see Maryla fondling the soft, white fur of a she-dog. She had just bathed her big, curly, Saint Bernard, Aza. She brushed Aza's silky hair. Gently, lovingly, she rested her forehead against

Aza's huge head. Maryla's usually furrowed forehead was now smoother, like the surface of the river on a windless summer morning when the river sits still—unruffled, younger, gentler.

"Aza, Azunia, Azenka, Azka . . ." I could still hear Maryla's voice speaking caressingly to the animal. I could see her long bony fingers sinking through the white hair.

After our arrival in Zabkowice, Maryla kept bringing home stray dogs. One day she found a starving dachshund with sad eyes, drooping ears, and a brown elongated torso resting on short, curved piano-like legs. Maryla named him Lapa (leg). Lapa proved quite useful. We had rats in the basement in 1946, and Lapa hunted the rats fearlessly, often bringing his trophy for Maryla to see.

Aza, much larger than Lapa, didn't hunt. One day she tried to imitate Lapa but failed. She caught the rat by its tail, but the rat turned around and bit into Aza's chin. Whining, she ran into the dining room just when Maryla and Rysiu were eating dinner. Seeing Aza crawling onto the carpet with a live rat dangling from her chin, Rysiu shrieked in horror and ran away from the table.

Maryla put down her soupspoon, stood up from her chair, grabbed a heavy rolling pin, and hit the rat on its head. The dead vermin fell onto the woolen carpet, staining it with Aza's blood. Maryla washed Aza's chin as if she were a nurse tending a wounded soldier. Recalling that scene, I realized how much I missed Maryla and wanted to see her again.

I thought about Maryla again in a theater in Torun, watching a domestic drama in which a man quarreled with a woman. At precise intervals he repeated the same accusations, the same blows. Then the woman started to cry, and I thought of Maryla. I had never seen her cry. She must have had reasons to feel sorry for herself. In Lublin, dispossessed, sleeping on a narrow sofa in a rented room, she didn't complain that she had left her furnished apartment and all her possessions in Lwow. I looked at the actress dancing with her partner; she cried but later forgave the man, like Maryla forgave Rysiu. But I couldn't forget how Maryla stood by Rysiu when he mistreated me.

Today, looking back, I think that they didn't realize how miserable I was. They were both simple uncomplicated people; I guess Rysiu's own childhood made him harder. Used to harsh treatment, he didn't know how to be gentle until he had his own children.

At that time, even my roommates' smoking brought memories of Maryla's face in the middle of the night: straight nose, smooth forehead, strong shoulders, long neck, strong chin, mouth with a cigarette. Filled with regrets, I wanted to see Maryla at once, but I didn't have any money to travel.

When I came to Bydgoszcz I received a small scholarship, but later our financial support was reduced to only room and board. For a while I didn't have any money, not even to buy ink or postage stamps or soap.

One Sunday afternoon, one among eight loud, laughing girls walking along a sidewalk, I heard my name called:

"Panno Marysiu!"

"Pan Porucznik!"

"Did you know that Rysiu and Maryla moved to Krakow?"

This man from Zabkowice gave me Maryla's new address in Krakow. During a winter recess I got a part in a children's play and bought a train ticket with my earnings. In the spring of 1952, I went to visit Maryla. By the time I stepped from the train in Krakow I had left behind my resentments. Maryla greeted me warmly. We didn't talk about the past. I played with her daughter, Krysia, and read books to her son, Julek. With her permed and bleached hair she looked different than I remembered. But I couldn't forget how she had treated me. Seeing Maryla with her own children made it even harder. I visited her again, but I couldn't forget how I suffered.

"Why did Maryla take you?" people always ask.

I don't know. According to Cesia, the Jewish woman who left me at Maryla's apartment, Maryla initially didn't know that I was Jewish. At the start of my journey, I probably looked appealing. My eight-year-old's face was still soft from my parents' love. Later, I wasn't that endearing anymore. In 1944, as a tense, thin, ragged girl, I lost my appeal.

On the night train, Cesia told Maryla about a husband who didn't like children. Perhaps Maryla would have acted differently had she known that I was Jewish. Yet, after taking me, she didn't turn me away.

Maryla was a handsome woman: tall, strong, long legged. In my mind's eye I see her in beige trousers and tall, shiny, black leather boots, walking briskly with a brown valise or standing by a window, looking out before making her next move, holding a cigarette in her bony fingers. She appeared tough, but she must have been scared often. Yet, once she took me she carried through her rescue.

As a young girl Maryla left her village to seek work in the city. Before the war, she married Jasiu, a handsome dark man who worked in a factory in Lwow. After the Germans sent Jasiu away Maryla found he had a liaison with another woman. Maryla thought that she wouldn't be able to have children of her own since one of her Fallopian tubes had been removed. That prognosis proved false. Later, in Zabkowice, Maryla gave birth to two children: Julek and Krysia.

Hiding me proved much harder than she originally thought. Her act often lay open for anybody to see; my black hair gave me away. Anyone could have reported Maryla to the Germans. We took numerous train rides; on each train we could have happened upon an informer. At every train stop we could have been caught by a German patrol. Yet Maryla didn't abandon me.

"Why did Maryla allow Cesia to bring me to her apartment?" I ask my husband, Romek, while we talk about the war. It is March, 1995 and we are in our garden in Jackson. In 1969, prior to our departure from Poland, Romek met Maryla in Krakow.

"I do not know; I suspect there was a mixture of more than one thing. She wasn't sure. Even today, if you were to ask her, she wouldn't know," says Romek. "Remember that it was a time of trial and turmoil. Several factors were at work here. Cesia was one of them. Maryla, who as a smuggler lived in the atmosphere of camaraderie, acted spontaneously. On the night train, in a dark compartment, she met another handsome woman. Cesia was also strong, also risk taking, and also lonely.

"There was also the practical side to it. At that time having a girl at home meant to have a maid. It was quite natural to expect that you would work. It was natural to want to have help at home."

I don't know why Maryla saved my life. Today, Tuesday, March 7, 1995, while the melting snow pours rivulets down the slope, uncovering my garden, and the passing cars splash mud over my sidewalk, I have only questions. I don't have a pretty story to tell, and I shrink from hearing nice clean stories.

On my journey from hiding to openness I must open all the doors, even the unpleasant ones. Harsh, even austere toward me, Maryla didn't spare herself either. Always busy, she worked hard without complaining. I don't recall seeing her at rest, or lounging around, or idling. Confused, I didn't know why she always found faults in me. I didn't behave like a girl. I was always reading. For her, reading books was a waste of time. Yet, once she took me she courageously cared for me; she risked her life for me, and she didn't give up.

Learning piece by piece, I went from not wanting to know, from trying to forget, from leaving everything at once, from not wanting to remember, from discarding the past like unwanted rummage, to a search taken up too late, without a map, with no guideposts and no directions, to slow and painful discoveries. Some pebbles fit the mosaic.

It is a circular motion. Again and again I go to the river to learn from scattered pebbles. I don't know why Maryla saved my life. I don't know why I didn't search for my family. For four years after the war I lived at the brutal edge of Rysiu's anger. When I left them I felt rejected. I kept away for three years; then, I went back. But I couldn't forget my pain.

Years later, I paid tribute to Maryla's courage. From my home in Jackson I wrote a letter to Yad Vashem, the Martyrs' and Heroes' Remembrance Authority in Israel, and in 1994 my Christian rescuer, Maryla, was named "Righteous among the Nations." She received a medal for saving my life during the war. A tree with Maryla's name will grow in Yad Vashem's Forest of the Righteous.

Take Back

In 1955 I took a train to Lodz, where I was born and lived as a child. This large industrial city was not destroyed in the war. The city hall where, in 1933, Tobiasz Winter had registered his daughter, Miriam, on the day of her birth stood intact. But I didn't search for my birth certificate. For all those years I used my false papers with a name not mine. Not Winter. Not Miriam. Why?

The theater school was not far away from the street where I once lived with my parents. The house where my mother sang Yiddish lullabies still stood on Nowomiejska Street. But I didn't listen to her cries. I didn't try to find my street. I didn't want to connect with my past, and I don't know why.

Since 1944, when Maryla had registered me in Lwow as Maria Bronislawa Dudek, born in Lwow in 1937, I had kept my false name. It went from one school certificate to the next, and I felt no remorse. When I left Maryla in 1948 I corrected my false birth date but didn't return to my name. As Maria—a formal version of Marysia—I married Romek in 1963 and moved to Lodz again. Even then, I didn't search for my documents. Not until 1969, just before leaving Poland. Not earlier.

———

TRAINS

On the day of my exam, I entered a large room with a parquet floor and tall, curtainless windows. There, I faced a long table at which the screening committee was seated.

"What poems did you prepare?" asked an older actress with graying blonde hair combed back into a chignon. I said, "'A Country Orphan,' by Maria Konopnicka, and 'Ab Urbe Condita,' by Julian Tuwim."

Reciting "Ab Urbe Condita," a poetic tribute to a Warsaw street peddler who makes the ruined city come alive with her selling calls, I recalled my own ride through the rubble on the army truck in the winter of 1945. I lost my stage fright and felt I was on a street again. When I called out loudly, "Buy fresh pastries!" I felt my coarse voice as if I stood again on a corner, selling. My body remembered the tray filled with Rysiu's tea cakes. I felt the chill of the morning, and half scared, half brazen, I called sharply:

"Do swiezego ciasta!" (buy fresh pastries).

"Tell me about your favorite role," said another actress, and I told her about the laughing tiger from the puppet show.

"Do you remember any lines?"

"Catastrophe!" I screamed, in the voice of the tiger who never lost his grin even when bringing bad news.

Take Back

"Why do you smile if the news is so bad?" I asked, mimicking Jadwiga's imitation of a toy's childlike voice.

"It's not my fault that they molded my face into a permanent smile," I said as a tiger again. Then, a young actor sitting by the window asked me to improvise a scene. "Go to get water from a well. Walk to the well with an empty bucket, then carry on with a heavy one. Forget about us watching you; use your imagination; do it silently; express any action through your body, changing your attitude as you go," he explained. "Behave as if you are holding an object; let us feel the weight of the water. Let us see where you are."

Stepping onto the stage, I inhaled the air of Wola Rzedzinska. I picked up the imaginary, empty, wooden bucket, opened the door of Maslowa's hut, and stepped over the high wooden threshold. Outside, mindful of the gander, I looked around. I didn't see any geese, so I walked briskly over the grass. I attached my bucket to the wooden arm of the well, the same way I had done it so often in Wola Rzedzinska during the war. I poured the water into my pail and looked around. The path leading back to the house was clear. I walked back carrying the heavy bucket. Then I heard a hiss, and a real fear crept into my steps.

Although in my entry exam I recalled a real scene from my former life, I didn't connect with my past

181

in any other way at all. In that small theater school with only ninety students, where we spent all of our time together and knew a lot about each other, I didn't tell anyone about myself. We rehearsed, worked on scenes, acted in plays, laughed. I had an easy smile that fit my face.

Our dormitory, called *Dom Akademicki* (academic house), was located in Baluty, a dilapidated part of the city with old run-down buildings without central heating. In the winter, we pooled our money to pay the janitor to keep the fire in our heating stove, since we left the dorm early in the morning and didn't return until late at night.

Three double bunk beds lined two walls of our room; two other single beds stood by the third wall. At night, crowded into a small room with eight beds, a table, a wardrobe, and a heating stove, eight girls gossiped, told jokes, and shared secrets. But I didn't reveal anything to my friends, to my diary, or to myself. I laughed, played, discussed, and argued, but I hid my past. I added more details to the invented, false story that I passed off as my past. I disguised those facts from my past that could identify me as a Jew. To cover my hiding during the war, I lied that I went to school. "I lived in Lwow with my aunt who worked in the post office." Concealing the murder of my family, I said that my parents died before the war. "My mother died at my birth; my father died of pneumonia." I lived my false life as if I were watching a film.

The theater school was housed on the first floor of an elegant villa previously owned by a wealthy manufacturer, Poznanski. On the second floor was the music conservatory. A large ballroom had been converted into a theater. Past the stage right was a long corridor where we sat on the floor waiting for our classes to start. At the end of that corridor was a library. Our librarian was rarely there. We used to pound at the door when we needed a book. He would pin short messages to the library door: "I left only for a moment."

"No, you are never here," we would write underneath his note. We could walk directly onto the stage from this long dark corridor.

Once, during a final examination, Richard Siodmak, a boyish, slender actor, played the role of an unjustly imprisoned boy in William Saroyan's *Hello, Out There.* The boy's cries were translated into Polish as "Is anybody there?" We sat, deeply moved by his helpless shouts. In the middle of Richard's performance, when he cried out louder, *"Is anybody there?"* we heard a hoarse voice backstage, and at the same time a tall, slightly bent figure appeared on stage: "What's it all about? I am here!" Our librarian thought that "Is anybody there?" had to be a call for him. It could have been a call for me as well.

In 1956, an acting student, Hanka Grodzienska, left Poland to join her newly found family in Canada. I knew that, like me, Hanka had spent part of her life in an orphanage. I also knew that, unlike me, she had been in a Jewish orphanage and that she was able to locate some relatives through the help of the Jewish community. Yet, I still didn't try to find out what happened to my family. Nothing could penetrate the thick shell under which I hid from myself.

In school, for my directing project in 1955, I dramatized a short story by Tadeusz Borowski in which a Jew is hunted by the Germans. I gave realistic stage directions to Slawek, the student actor cast in the role of the hunted man. But I didn't see that as my own life played out on the stage. I didn't feel myself running through a forest. I didn't think of my own fear and exhaustion.

Only sometimes, unexpectedly, I cried when no one could see me: in the theater, in the movies, when the lights were out.

Caught unprepared, I cried watching a film with my roommate, Nina. On the screen I saw a Jewish family thrown into a street, the grandfather's hat torn from his head, smashed by a passing car. Seized by loud, violent sobs, I couldn't stop crying. People in the cinema looked surprised at my behavior, but I kept sobbing. Nina put her arm on my shoulder. I can't say for sure if she squeezed my hand. I think that she did, but I didn't respond. Afterward I behaved toward Nina, my roommate who showed me compassion, as if nothing had happened.

————

Much had occurred in Poland during those four years. When in the fall of 1955 I entered the theater school, the Communists' regime held a tight grip over art. In our declamation class we recited political speeches. Then came the thaw. What happened in school was overshadowed by the events of 1956.

Take Back

Wednesday, April 4, 1956
Trybuna Ludu prints more articles about the injustices committed by the Communist regime. Why did we believe all those lies?

Sunday, May 6, 1956
Where is the truth? It is always hidden. We never know all the facts. Knowing only a fraction, we think that we comprehend. What's more, we passionately believe and then, when the truth comes out, we feel deceived.

Monday, October 28, 1956
Our Soviet friends bloodied the streets of Budapest. How can we stay calm and watch without doing anything? How can I go on dissecting a play about Mazepa, while the Soviet tanks stand waiting at the outskirts of Lodz? What difficult times we happen to live in. It's impossible to just watch.

In 1956 I directed *Mother*, a short play from Jerzy Szaniawski's *Two Theaters,* a play about words that meant something else. Later, in my diary, I considered Henrik Ibsen's *Peer Gynt:*

TRAINS

Sunday, May 26, 1957
Peer Gynt; and my life. Mirages, illusions, and an incessant escape from reality . . . Have I ever known how to be myself? Haven't I worn countless, deceiving masks? How many have I had? How many times have I changed my own principles? Now only emptiness, a frightening void. Peer Gynt threw away principles. He followed his impulses without thinking, without control. Looking back at the end of the play, he concluded that he had wasted his life. And I, who seemingly proceeded with self-control, have arrived at the same sorry balance.

—————

After graduation I took trains again: I moved from Lodz to Kielce, from Kielce to Warsaw. Through a mutual friend I met Romek.

Until Romek asked me, "How did your mother call you?" I didn't tell anybody about myself. "How did your mother call you?" he repeated, and I repeated, "Marysia." I didn't tell him the truth. I showed him my mask when he wanted to see my face. But he persisted, and finally I told him the truth and fell in love with this man who could make me real.

From the moment I whispered *Mirka* to Romek and he called my real name, we belonged to each other. It was as if I'd known him all my life. As if he had given me back my heart. He called loudly, *Mirka*, so loudly that he awakened his siblings sleeping in the next room.

But I couldn't let go of my fears. In 1962 Romek invited me to spend the Christmas holiday at his mother's house. *A house in the woods so secluded and safe*, I thought, entering the small thatched hut. Later, when we were trying to leave Poland, I thought again about that house as a suitable hiding place for our young son, Daniel.

Only after Romek made me admit that I was Jewish did my mask slide from my face. I felt as if someone had shown me the real me. Until then, I steadfastly clasped my false name. Until then I kept my mask intact; rosy-hued, quick-witted, joking, bristling with adventure, good-humored, loudly laughing, I appeared on the surface as if my scale of perception ranged from a joke to a joke. Still keeping my true feelings to myself, I laughed often and loudly, but on the margin of that laughter rang confusion not heard by anyone, not even by me. Then, Romek and I married in April of 1963.

Even then, I didn't name myself truthfully. My marriage certificate shows Maria Dudek as my maiden name. Even after Romek forced me to tell him the truth, I didn't let other people know that I was Jewish. Then, I blew up.

In 1967 articles in the Polish press made me fearful again. One day, during a meeting in the Lodz Culture House, where I worked, Pani Basia, my supervisor, recalled seeing a Jewish boy searching for food in a garbage pile. She said:

"It happened in 1942, during the war. We could see him through the window. He held a red pot, methodically searching the garbage."

TRAINS

I saw my brother. I couldn't sleep. I was haunted by the image of a boy scavenging for food. All I could see was a garbage pail and a starving little boy, a small red pot in his hand, thin fingers clasped around the red enamel handle. Mourning my murdered brother, I imagined his small body, burnt, parched, charred, and couldn't stop crying.

During the Arab-Israeli conflict that led to the 1967 Six Day War the Polish government took the side of the Arabs and condemned Israel. The government-owned press continued an anti-Jewish campaign. Every day I read articles condemning Jews.

Fearful for other children, charged with emotions I couldn't control, I thought about the starving little boy from the garbage dump, my brother, Jozio, my son, Daniel, our friend's son, Dan. In my mind those images merged into one.

Jozio and Daniel and Dan. Romek's Jewish friends, Zenka and Kuba, left Poland in 1956. Their son, Dan, was born in Israel in 1962, two years earlier than our son, Daniel. So, from Israel to Poland Zenka sent packages with things too small for her son to wear. What their Dan outgrew our Daniel wore. Daniel used to sit on the balcony of our third floor apartment in Lodz, looking down at the passersby, his tiny fists holding the wrought iron posts. Often, he'd throw down from the balcony his multicolored visor hat, red, orange, and cornflower blue.

"What a darling hat," a stranger would say at the door, handing me the hat, which Zenka had sent for Daniel.

And then it happened. I read the articles condemning Jews and feared for the lives of Jewish

children. Zenka's son, Dan, whose hat colored our
balcony had become for me like my brother, Jozio.
Mourning Jozio, haunted by an image of a boy
searching a pile of kitchen refuse, at first I cried
silently, and then, one day, I exploded.
On that day Z. sat with a group of
instructors when I entered his office to return a file.
The Polish government had condemned Israel, and
in a smoke-filled room Z. discussed with other
instructors the war between Israel and the Arab
states. When I entered he asked:
"Whose side are you on?"
"I am on the side of my people."
"Good answer," said Z. I knew that Z. was a
government informer.
He didn't know that I was Jewish. I told
him. That was the first time that I publicly said:
"I am Jewish. I fear for the safety of the
Jewish children. They may be killed again. I am
Jewish," I repeated. I had never said this before.
Why did I correct that informer when I
realized that he misunderstood me? Why did I let
those people know that I was Jewish at a time
when Jews were being persecuted again? Was that
long, loud, mournful admission a substitution for a
funeral rite for my murdered brother, Jozio?
Until then, scorched, hardened, insensitive,
I didn't face my past. Until then I kept my mask
intact. I rolled along. I hugged the road like a well-
made wheel. I spun through the dust. I steered
through the sleet and drove smoothly over the
glossy asphalt of my lies. Now I turned into an
unwieldy wagon. My mask fell off like a hubcap,
with a rusty howling yell. The hub cracked, the

spokes of lies fell off, and the wheel couldn't roll anymore.

Maybe this loud howling call had been growing inside me since the time that I left my family and let them be killed alone. I didn't know, but I had to scream out:

"Look at me. I, too, should have been killed. I am Miriam Winter!"

———

Then we emigrated, but not until we got three rejections. First, my superiors gave me a chance to replace the mask or be fired.

"Write a letter to the newspaper condemning the Jews and you can stay in your job."

I refused, and so I was dismissed from work in the Culture House. We asked for permission to emigrate, but since Romek wasn't Jewish they wouldn't let him go.

There was no legal emigration from Poland then, but through a strange twist of international politics I, as a Jew, could leave, but my husband, a Pole, could not. I knew that Romek would be punished if I left him behind, yet I didn't want to stay in Poland. I felt powerless; my life was over. I'd never teach or direct again; we'd be imprisoned; Daniel would have to live parentless like his mother did.

Take Back

Out of work, confined to our apartment, I waited on the margin of reality. Even walking the street, I felt nonexistent. Former acquaintances looked away, pretending not to know me. Voices on the radio condemned the Jews. I'd listen to a polka played on the radio and I'd bounce to its beat with Daniel, but the music would stop to give way to another hateful speech. So I'd give a toy car to my son, and I'd stare at our rejection papers.

Romek wanted to escape. In Krakow lived Zenek, my friend from the orphanage. He worked in the customs department certifying things shipped out from Poland. So, Romek went to Krakow to speak with Zenek:

"Ship me out in some parcel."

"The only way you could go would be in a transport of meat; you'd freeze to death."

We reapplied, anticipating another rejection. I went around asking for help; some former friends promised to intervene discreetly. We stood in lines again to submit our applications.

One morning while we stood in line, Romek said loudly: "You don't have any documents stating that you are Jewish. Who would believe you that you are Miriam Winter born in Lodz?"

"Did you search for your papers in the city hall?" asked an old man who had overheard Romek's loud speech. I looked back. The man had a wrinkled face and soft brown eyes.

"No, I didn't search."

"Then, go to the city hall. If you were born in Lodz, you should find your papers. Lodz wasn't burned during the war." His eyes darkened, but he spoke softly, as one speaks to a child.

TRAINS

Two hours later, Romek found my papers in the city hall. I looked down at the copy of my birth certificate. For the first time since the war, in 1969, I saw my true name, Miriam Winter, on an official document. I was born in Lodz in 1933. I came back to Lodz in 1955. I walked the streets; I had all the time in the world. Yet, it had never occurred to me to look for my papers. Now I held them in my trembling hand, the first proof of my identity.

Romek also found the birth certificate of my little brother, Jozio, born on February 5, 1938. I touched my eyelids. It was hard to read through the tears. Until that cold afternoon on January 1969, I didn't know how old Jozio was when I left him in Ozarow, in 1941. I thought, he was three. When we walked together, I didn't have to stoop to hold his little hand. But I wasn't sure. Now I knew.

Looking at my papers filled by hand in a careful, schoolgirl's penmanship, I felt new blood flowing through my fingers. Outside my window, the street noise blended into a sound of train. I touched the names of Tobjasz and Majta-Laja and Jozef—my little Jozio— and Miriam.

Finally the permission to emigrate came. We left Poland on May 14, 1969. I have never gone back.

Italy, 1969

I had my first pizza in Rome in the spring of 1969. Waiting for permission to enter the United States, we spent almost half a year in Rome. At last, after three rejections, we were out of Poland: displaced, stateless, but free. We lived in one room, with our son Daniel, waiting for the signal to go. Where? We didn't know. Who would allow us to come to their country? We waited to find out.

Waiting for our documents to be processed, our past checked, our identity confirmed, immensely happy to be out of Poland, we befriended Romans and learned to speak Italian. We'd walk to Piazza and Porta Maggiore. We'd stop at a sidewalk cafe. At night we watched fire-eaters on Piazza Navona and drank young wine with our landlady, Ghina.

There was nothing to do but wait. To leave Poland we had to give up our citizenship. Stateless, we couldn't work. We got a loan from a Jewish organization that we repaid later in small installments, after settling in the United States.

All through that summer we laughed more, sang louder than ever before, splashing our happiness over the fountains of Rome. On the Square of the Republic we'd touch the naiad for good luck, not knowing where we would go, yet carefree, exhilarated, drunk with freedom.

Those twenty-three weeks in Rome were among the happiest in my life. There were no surprises; long before leaving Poland we knew that as refugees from a Communist country we would have to wait but, unlike my sorrowful wait in Poland, when I thought that we'd never get out, this waiting put me at ease. I felt soft, playful, easy as the Italian summer sun that shone splendidly every day.

Daniel's wooden toys rattled in his backpack when we boarded the train in Warsaw. He kept his favorite toy car in his pocket; I carried his books and more cars in my tote. Our books traveled by sea in a crate tightly packed with lamps, pictures, glassware, pots and pans. One wooden crate, not much taller than my five foot frame, protected our belongings behind its waterproof lining.

We arrived in Rome with one valise and one duffel bag. For one week we lived in a small hotel on Porta Maggiore. On the first night we stood on the balcony watching the city. Below, a white-clad policeman in a white helmet directed traffic. His white-gloved arms moved like a dance, while cars like Daniel's toys circled the lighted piazza.

At dinnertime, Daniel sat at the table unwilling to eat. He gaped at the TV screen in the corner of the dining room, hoarding food in his mouth. Carlo, the owner, a stout, bold man, turned the TV off.

"No mangiare, no televisione."

Italy, 1969

Daniel's eyes filled with tears. He moved his mouth once or twice, trying to eat, but as soon as Carlo turned the TV on, his face returned to a food-hoarding stupor. Then, Carlo served pizza, which Daniel liked. The first bite, crisp and hot, unlike anything I'd eaten before, still lingers in my mouth when I think of Rome.

———

From the first morning when he greeted us at the train station upon our arrival from Vienna, Rysiek was our *Cicerone*, our guide through Rome. Rysiek, an architect who had come to Rome a month earlier, gave us some quick pointers:

"If you had Latin in high school you'll understand Italian," said Rysiek. "Look for a sign in the window: *camera a cuccina,* signaling a room with a shared kitchen. A kitchen without refrigerator would be cheaper, but you'd need to be close to the market, to shop every day." Rysiek drew a circle on the map of Rome, and we rented a room on via Principe Umberto, *numero quatro sette* (47), near the train station *(stazione termini).*

There, Daniel befriended Claudio, an Italian boy, who lived on the second floor. We lived another floor up. Claudio had a red bicycle that Daniel wanted to ride. Soon Claudio shared his bicycle and played with Daniel's cars.

TRAINS

Every morning I'd take Daniel to the market on Piazza Emanuele Vittorio. Holding Daniel's hand I looked at tables and stalls set amid remains of that Rome I knew from history books. We passed broken columns, pieces of marble, stones that once were pedestals, capitols, statues. We'd come early, walking between the stalls, observing how the merchants worked unloading, unpacking, setting out, hanging, arranging, displaying their cheese, fish, poultry, flowers, barrels, baskets, wooden crates, fresh grapes, eggplants, onions, oranges, lemons.

There were things to touch and smell. I'd bend over the orange flesh of a freshly cut melon that smelled like a promise to keep. I touched an oblong eggplant, tight like a baby's cheek. On hot days, long sprigs of basil smelled like a cool, shaded garden.

Early in the morning I watched how the sellers decorated their stalls with all kinds of grapes. Scattered on a table, grapes lay in wait. Later, garlands of grapes circled wooden poles, graced tall urns, and hung from the edge of the table. More grapes hung from metal wires. Garlands of green and yellow, large and purple, small, round, dark red. Large purple grapes unlike those I knew from Poland; all kinds of grapes stockpiled in baskets; small and round, oblong and large, luscious, lurking behind dark-green leaves while my mouth watered.

I looked for things I knew from Poland: carrots, potatoes, onions. I'd buy beets, cucumbers, and tomatoes. But even the vegetables I knew held surprises in every stall. There were all kinds of beans: pale yellow, creamy white, dark green, short and rounded, long and thick, narrow, elongated, broad, displayed in tall baskets under a canopy of grapes. I knew one kind of tomato, round and red, but here tomatoes came in all shapes: some as small as a cherry, others huge as a freshly dug potato, still another, a plumlike oval. Their colors ranged from yellows to purples with even the reds tinted from light orange to deep, dark red.

Some days I'd get food that I hadn't known before. One day I bought anchovies from a dark wooden barrel that smelled of the sea. I liked the pungent salty taste in my mouth, but Romek didn't like it, so I never bought another anchovy while in Rome. I had a dollar and a half a day to feed the three of us. One dollar exchanged for 618 lira, and I calculated our expenses, counting the coins in whatever denomination.

We didn't have squash in Poland; I had never even seen one until that summer in Rome. I wondered how would I cook one, how would it taste, but with Daniel and Romek both fussy eaters, I didn't take any chances. I only bought what I knew my family would eat. I paid twenty lira for one banana, which Daniel ate while we walked back. Then, I'd go to the bakery to buy fresh bread and then to a store next door to buy milk in a triangular carton.

In Poland we carried our own milk bottle to the store. We also boiled the milk in Poland, mindful of tuberculosis, which could be spread from the cows. Not aware that modern pasteurization killed the germs, I continued boiling milk in Rome.

Once Beata, Zenka's sister whom Romek had known in Poland and who now lived in New York City, came to visit. She didn't stay long (Rome was only a part of her European tour), but she went grocery shopping and gave me a few pointers.

"American kids love cold cereal," said Beata, pointing to one: Kellogg's cornflakes.

The next morning I put the crunchy flakes into Daniel's bowl and boiled the milk. Then, I poured hot milk into Daniel's bowl. The crunchy cereal turned into a soft, pulpy, sticky colorless mush.

Later, I took Daniel to "the mouth of truth" (*bocca della verita*), a primitive large stony circle with an opening that looked like a mouth. The ancient Romans believed that the stone would bite off one's hand if one told a lie. I frightened Daniel by telling him the legend as if it was the truth.

When little, Daniel had Romek's blond hair. Even today Daniel's hair is only slightly brown, like burned amber, and his younger brother's reddish brown, like oak leaves in winter. In Rome, Daniel's hair attracted   the attention of the dark-haired Italians.

"Come vi chiamate?"

"Daniel."

"Oh, Daniele. Quanti anni hai?"

Daniel showed four fingers.

"Quattro."

On June 21, 1969, Daniel turned five, and I gave him a birthday party in our small bedroom. I served a Wedel's torte, a dry, round, chocolate and wafer confection that my friend Baska pushed through the train's window on our departure from Poland on May 14, 1969.

My friends came to the train station to say good-bye. Did they know that we would never meet again? Adam, my friend from Lodz, gave me a miniature silver candelabra that could be fitted with five small birthday candles and said:

"Remember our long nightly talks."

Adam paraphrased a verse from the great Polish romantic poet, Adam Mickiewicz, words suggesting soul searching, late at night, colored by saying things not allowed to be heard in the daylight: "Poles' long nightly debates . . ." sharing dangers, dreams, doubts, youthful heroism.

When I placed this miniature candelabra on top of my torte and lighted the candles, Rysiek remarked that this birthday arrangement epitomized our existence in Rome: dry, tightly packed (all belongings under the bed in one valise), yet still burning, like the candles on top of a child's cake.

We were like this expensive, elaborately decorated box, designed by Baska, my artist friend, for a chocolate factory. A box with a cake inside, a torte, made only for export, rarely obtained by a Polish shopper, and therefore having a taste of rare luxury. Out of place in this crowded bedroom, displaced, tight, and ready to go on short notice.

"To the future," said Rysiek, when a bottle of Polish vodka (a gift from Tomek, my husband's childhood friend) went around the room.

We drank Tomek's vodka in our rented room with other displaced stateless people, waiting for our papers to be processed, our diplomas translated, our pasts investigated, our identities checked, confirmed.

TRAINS

———

Rysiek and his wife, Linka, encouraged us to hitch rides on Italian roads. We often traveled together. Their daughter, Kaska, played with Daniel. Hitchhiking we went to Vesuvius, Pompei, and Capri.

The best pizza, according to Daniel, was at the market in Sienna. Daniel ate his pizza in front of a stall piled with music boxes, fascinated with a ballerina on top of one carved wooden box inlaid with glittering glass. The glass beads reflected the high noon sun, Daniel's white hat, and the blue sky above. The ballerina, in white, on top of the box, turned slowly. I looked at Daniel's cheeks red from pizza, ignoring his soiled white shirt. Dark-red tomato sauce dripped around his mouth, his lips, his knees.

"You can't keep a little boy clean," said Linka.

———

Only once, on a usually busy turnpike running from Naples to Genoa, were we unable to hitch a ride. On the Sunday of July 21, 1969, the highway was empty. We didn't know that the whole world was watching American astronauts landing on the moon.

Finally, a truck full of grapes stopped and we got on. Anthony, the driver, a strong man with broad shoulders, short, even shorter than Romek, opened the door smiling, as if he had just met long-lost friends on the empty road. I noticed his heavy eyelids when he let us in.

Anthony kept hitting his wrists against the steering wheel. I kept Daniel on my lap, Romek sat close to Anthony and talked with him nonstop all the way to Rome, asking questions about his cargo, his bambino, his wife, Rosa, his brother, Phillippo.

Anthony transported grapes from Sicily to Genoa, about 1800 miles on the road, a forty-eight-hour drive. Even on a normal day *La strada Del Sole* (the sunny highway), which ran in a straight line across the Italian boot, could lull a commuter to sleep. Now virtually empty, the road was frightfully boring in the glaring sun. He stopped for us because he was falling asleep after forty-eight hours of eating in the car, of driving without a break to sleep, of stopping only when absolutely necessary. He swore angrily against the Sicilian mafia, whom he called *comandantes*, who paid little to the truck drivers.

Strada didn't run to Rome, but clearly afraid of falling asleep on an empty highway and grateful for our presence, Anthony brought us to the outskirts of Rome, and we concluded our trip by electric train.

TRAINS

Rysiek and Linka left Rome earlier than we did.
When their visa arrived, we had supper together.
On that night, on via Giolitti, on our way to the
pizzeria, we heard singing, then shouts and
screams, and were almost trampled by a crowd
when we reached Piazza della Republica. There, on
the first anniversary of the Soviet invasion of
Czechoslovakia, amid the lighted baroque fountains
of tritons and nymphs, modernity clashed with the
past.

Italian Communists marched and shouted;
their slogans, carried on large wooden boards,
reminded us of why we were in Rome.

Later that night, watching the owner as he
shoveled pizza into the brick oven, we thought of
parting, and the room smelled of garlic, oregano,
and Chianti.

"Tutti Auguri Dottore!" Ghina, our landlady,
called from another table covered with a checkered
red and white cloth.

"Where should we send our letters?" asked
Rysiek, whose uncle lived in Denver. We still didn't
know where we would go, but we wanted to keep in
touch. Daniel wanted to know whether we would
have pizza after leaving Rome.

Then, summer ended and Ghina brought us
good news.

Italy, 1969

"Dottore telefonare!" she called, running up the marble stairs.

When Romek told me that we could go to Boston, I leaped into a wild victory dance. I swirled around the marble kitchen floor, singing wildly about a train taking us to Boston. Daniel came to the kitchen when he heard my screams.

"We shall take a train to Boston," I said.

"You can't ride a train over the ocean," said Daniel.

"So we'll fly first and then take the train to Boston," said Romek, and we joined hands and circled the floor. Then, inventing trainlike steps, discovering trainlike sounds, arms over each other's shoulders, we sped about Ghina's kitchen floor. Three pairs of legs pretending to hit a train's metal tracks: choo-choo, cha . . . choo choo cha . . . To Boston, to Boston, choo . . . choo . . . cha . . . I danced with my husband and son. I moved my arms and legs, expressing the movements of a train as I did years ago when I recited Tuwim's "Locomotive," in a clandestine classroom in the Warsaw Ghetto. Arms forward and back like the piston rods: *buch, uch, puff, uff,* stepping into the gradually increasing rhythm of a train, hitting my heels hard like wheels hit the track: to tak-toto, tak-toto, tak-toto tak . . . But now, I tapped to the beat of freedom: tatata, tatata, tatata . . . Filled with joy, we traveled around the room: to Boston, to Boston, choo . . . choo . . . Romek put two fingers into his mouth and whistled like a train, and with another loud choo chooo choooo . . . we sped away.

"I hope they have pizza there," said Daniel.

TRAINS

On parting, Ghina put a can of tomatoes and a chunk of parmesan cheese into Daniel's backpack:

"Pomodoro, Parmigiano." Then, Ghina kissed Daniel and we flew away. *"Ciao Bambino!"* she called, waving good-bye.

———

In October 1969 we flew out of Italy and settled in the United States. I have found my place.

Epilogue

The taste of honey still lingers in my mouth as I take my red shovel to clean the driveway. It is early morning in winter 1996. Outside the day starts bright and crisp. Tree branches leafless, almost black, contrast with the white, snow-covered garden. Everything is clear, well-defined, black and white. No gray.

In less than two hours I will tell my story. Again, some questions I'll answer with, "I don't know." Like the one about Maryla's motives for saving my life. Driving to Ann Arbor, just a forty-mile stretch on Interstate 94, I think about those gray, unanswered questions.

When I left Poland at age thirty-six, in 1969, I didn't think that I'd be able to function in another language. But my two sons—David, who was born in Boston in 1970, and his brother, Daniel—taught me English, while I worked in a store and took classes at night. Later, I taught acting to American students. I directed *Antigone* and *Ondine* and *Peer Gynt* in an American college. Then, I went back to school. At fifty-nine, in 1992, I earned a Ph.D. in theater from Michigan State University.

TRAINS

But my trip to Ann Arbor isn't about theater. Today, I will tell my story to students at the University of Michigan. Maybe that's why I survived, to tell what happened. I am a witness. I have to reclaim the dead from the death of nonremembrance.

Walk with me
by a railroad track
step by step
back

back to a last
childish game
tough the night
ride the train

train your eye
tear by tear
to see the night
to hear

steps on the track
cries unheard
step on the rail
this train
won't come back
back

Epilogue

Trying to find the facts of my past and the truth behind the facts, I write. In the car while driving, in the morning in a corner of my room, in front of a computer, at strange tables, while waiting for my yoga class, while lined up in a supermarket, at breakfast with my friends after a Sunday walk. On a cold winter morning icicles hang from my eyelashes above a dark-blue, propylene ski mask when I walk in the park, but I don't hide behind the mask anymore.

I write on paper, on coffee-stained place mats, on a symphony ticket, on a dollar bill, on the back of my script, and on lined, loose pages of cheap filler paper. Sometimes, to prevent a stranger reading what I write, I write in Polish.

I list expressions that catch my ear, like Ann's saying "that's a keeper" while we taped a radio program, titled *Remnants*, based on memories of survivors. Almost everything is a keeper for me as I try to open the lock of my trunk; the rusted trunk of *nonremembrance*.

In *Remnants*, a play written by Hank Greenspan, I portrayed a woman who "sorted the clothes of those who had already been gassed and burned." During the rehearsal I kept a scarf on my knees. My hand touched the wool, trying to imagine my mother's brown sweater.

TRAINS

"Are you going to the Gathering of Child Survivors in Montreal?" asks a friend.

"Yes."

"We could share a room during the conference."

"That's a keeper," I say, folding my notes into the breast pocket of my parka.

Behind the window of my Chevrolet Cavalier, my eyes rest on the vastness of white. I see myself at age eleven, walking back home after a storm. Home? When Rysiu sent me out to sell pastries I missed the last train and spent the night walking during the storm. Why return after I missed the last train?

Maybe someone would have rescued me had I cried when Rysiu beat me. Instead, I pressed my teeth into the skin of my hand and kept silent. Why did I stay? A normal person would have run away. Wouldn't you?

Epilogue

Inside, a large auditorium is filled with students. They are nineteen, and twenty, and twenty-one. I stand in front of the map of Poland responding to their questions.

"Maybe not guilt," says an older man sitting on my left somewhere in the middle of this large auditorium when I say that I feel guilty for surviving. He hears my foreign accent, and he wants to help me find the right word.

But that's how I feel each time I see a photo of a child, like Jozio, in front of barbed wire. Guilty for being spared when others were killed. Guilty for surviving when my family didn't. I listen to the sound of the word *guilt*, and I can touch its slimy pulp. It holds like glue.

Afterward, in my parka, boots, and fuzzy, woolen gloves, I go for a walk. Wind makes my cheeks tingle. The road slopes uphill, and my feet begin to ache. I stop, stretch my hamstrings, and continue uphill. Now the questions blow in the wind: "Why didn't I search for my family?"

The snow falls on my face, soft and clean; young snow, just fallen, unspoiled, fresh and receptive. It smells like hope and trust. What happened to my feelings of trust? Why did I hide my Jewish identity after the danger was over?

I hear those questions in the snow under my feet as I walk back toward my car. I press my boot into the snow, and the snow shapes around the sole.

It's give-and-take. I squeeze a handful of snow; it takes the shape of my fingers. "Why did I stay so long with Maryla and Rysiu?"

That question is tangible, like the onion that I brought to the rehearsal when I directed Ibsen's *Peer Gynt.* It smells like an onion, but my tears are real. Peer Gynt ran away; why did I stay? I look at that question. I bring it to my nose and sniff like a dog. I am still in the middle of the campus. I pick up more snow and squeeze it in my palm. Now, even that handful of snow has a stinking smell.

Why didn't Maryla let me go? Why did she force me to stay in her abusive household for three years? Why didn't she let me go when those two Jews came to fetch me? Had I gone I would have been Jewish during my formative years.

Why did I let Maryla force me to stay? Once I had a choice. Why did I choose so badly? She said, "Now you are going to betray me like the Jews betrayed Jesus," and I chose to stay.

Alone, lonely, I missed the human touch. More than food or warmth I longed for a pat on my head. I watched Maryla when she cuddled her dogs. Why did I stay?

Driving back I let those questions cut into my heart. I scream in sudden bolts of anger. I cry behind the wheel. In Ozarow, my grandparents, my parents, and Jozio, the six of us, lived in one room. They called me Mirka. The harder it was for them to hide the fear, the more they cuddled me and my brother. Then one evening I went away, and no one touched me anymore. Even today I cry over the void. Like someone whose limb was cut off but who still feels the pain in the missing part. My missing part never ceased to hurt.

Epilogue

A lost limb. I feel this pain when a friend recalls her mother talking to her when she was eleven. I keep my mouth shut as I stumble in the park, but I want to scream. No one stroked my hair, and that part of my body still hurts.

Why was I so dumb? I needed help. At night, I put my fists into my mouth so as not to cry. Why didn't I ask for help? It would have been much better if I hadn't been so brave.

Why didn't she let me go? And the other people in town, teachers, priests, passersby, customers in the store, who heard Rysiu's abusive shouts and saw him beat me. Why didn't they intervene? They could hear his curses on the street in the small town.

When Maryla and Rysiu finally let me go I was fifteen years old. Why so late? I could have walked away. Why didn't I? What put my instincts to sleep? Why didn't I run? Any animal would. Unless I wanted to punish myself for surviving.

Maybe if I hadn't been so hard on myself, if I had allowed myself to cry and complain, if I had admitted to myself that I was unhappy, that my life was too hard for me, maybe I would have been a better mother for my two sons. But I hardened. I didn't acknowledge my own unhappiness, and then, I was unable to see when my children needed my love and understanding. I hid behind my mask. It made me stronger but untrue. I lived without a place to call my own. All I owned I kept in a small valise under my bed. Except for a bundle of books tied with a string, all my possessions fit snugly into that old valise.

TRAINS

Now, I strive to tell the truth. I listen to my heart and admit to less lofty feelings like uncertainty and fear and envy. I feel envious even during the gatherings of hidden children because I was so completely alone. Because no one talked with me about my situation. And because my life in hiding was so terribly complicated by the priest's refusal to baptize me.

That priest was probably a noble man. It would have been easier for him just to baptize me than to go through the charade. But why didn't he think what his refusal would do to a child who embraced his religion and for two more years, completely alone at nine, and ten, and eleven years old, a girl had to go with strangers to the church and each time go with them to confession and then pretend to take communion?

It was only after we left Poland, in 1969, that I began searching for my family. In 1971, I sent a letter to a Polish newspaper in Israel. I enclosed my birth certificate, which I had found in Lodz's city hall before we left Poland. I asked for help in locating any relatives, or anybody alive who may have known me. Cesia Weinlos, the brave Jewish woman who took me away from Ozarow, now lives in Israel. There, reading my name in a Polish newspaper, under the title *"KTO MNIE ZNA?"* (who knows me?) Cesia recognized the girl she once took from Ozarow. She wrote to me. Later, in 1980, we met in her home, in Israel.

In 1979, forty years after the war began; another newspaper ad helped me locate my cousin Celina, a survivor from the Lodz Ghetto. Celina was in the Lodz Ghetto with her parents, who perished. My uncle Szmulek, Celina tells me, also was in the Lodz Ghetto. His wife, Janka, gave birth to a baby boy, which was unusual, Celina tells me, because women there were too emaciated to become pregnant. "Janka was plump before the war; maybe that's why. But the boy was sickly; he cried a lot." Celina had known my parents and grandparents well. Her mother and my grandmother were cousins. "You look like Szmulek," she said when we met. "Your grandfather was a Hassid; his name was Szymon. We called your mother Lonka."

From such bits of information, I try to reconstruct my past. I collect the pieces, trying to assemble them into a composite.

"Did you know my parents?" I ask anyone who lived in Lodz before the war. Each bit of information, like a small pebble, finds its place in the mosaic.

TRAINS

"Do you believe in God?" asked my roommate when we sat together for *Shabbos* service during the Gathering of Child Survivors in Montreal in 1994.

"I believe in Jews praying together," I said. "I don't know whether God exists, but even if he doesn't, he is here."

Sitting among survivors who came from all over the world I felt his presence. God was with us *davening*, bending his knees, praying with the former hidden children of whom only so few survived. I looked at old people around me, but I only saw children trying to hide; Jewish boys and girls running scared; looking for the shelter that so few found. In this clean-smelling hotel room in Montreal where we gathered to pray, I smelled the ashes. I prayed that God did, too.

It was only much later, after arriving in the United States, that I returned to my Jewish religion. In the fall of 1969, still in Rome awaiting permission to enter the United States, we went to an old *Sephardic* synagogue. It was Rosh Hashanah, the Jewish New Year. Families stood together praying.

Epilogue

Each group was covered with a *tallis*, the Jewish prayer shawl. I looked at one family. In the center stood a tall man, covered with a *tallis*, spreading his arms over each member of his large family as if protecting his flock. The fringes of his *tallis* rested on the heads of two little girls at both ends of the sequence, so that his whole family seemed covered. The *tallis*, like a tent's roof, made me feel safe. I felt that I had returned to my own tent. I came back under the roof of my tent, and the floor of the synagogue was my ancient land covered with tents. I could remember that I was home. It was fall. I knew there would be other winters. I also knew there would be a *tallis* that would cover me. Safe. Home.

These are the houses I've known, the towns I remember, the tables I've moved among. One room is lost forever.

A small room, in the outskirts of town. A rented room in someone's else's house, in a strange town with a strange-sounding name, Ozarow. My family was transient there. It was a step on a flight of stairs. Yet it was a quiet room, tranquil despite the fears that were whispered by adults, whispered in foreign tongues to feign tranquility, to make children feel safe. In the center of the room was a small wooden table. Around that table four people sat, but I cannot see them anymore.

I can hear them chant; I don't know the tune. Their heads covered, Father and Grandfather, their eyes locked; a too-large hat on Jozio's tiny head. A room as small as the planet Earth dropped from God's hold . . .

———

Now, teaching acting in a small Midwestern town, I bring odd objects to class. My students find their true selves through tactile and sensual experience. Blindfolded, they open their senses; they touch, they smell, they hear. As they learn to be visually and aurally attentive they recapture the time when they were very young. We walk through my garden, smelling herbs; "I remember eating pizza during a trip to Petoskey," someone whispers, holding a green sprig of oregano. Sometimes during a walk bits of my past turn up unexpectedly.

During the war I cast off my senses. Hungry and cold, I learned to ignore my body as if it did not exist. I ignored my needs for rest, for shelter, and for comfort. From the age of eight until I was fifteen I lived in deprivation. I turned away from my body. Deprivation made me rigid and tense.

It wasn't until much later in my life that I began to learn again how to feel. Then, still later, I wanted to recall my past, but I couldn't. So, I asked my feelings to teach me how to remember. I began by asking questions. "How does it feel to touch a fur collar?" I asked myself while alone in a dark room. Then, slowly, some feelings talked back to me.

I asked, "How does my body respond to cold?" I remembered running in wooden clogs in winter. I remembered that the cold was most disturbing early in the spring. The combination of damp and wind made me shiver when I went to the clearing in the woods, gathering some new grass for the cow still kept in the barn.

Then, I remembered the warmth of fire and fur. I remembered returning to the warm corner of a room, the oven still hot after bread-baking; fire, warmth, burning wood; the smell of cooked cabbage; a pot of cabbage and beans in summer; sauerkraut and beans in winter. But to recover the smells of the time with my parents I have to recall *czulent*.

Czulent . . . baked in a red enamel pot. A dish of mostly potatoes and beef, baked overnight in a slow oven. *Czulent* is the sum and substance of my lost childhood: when I say the word aloud I can taste, touch, and smell its burned essence. On Saturday morning the smell of *czulent* filled our small rented room in Ozarow, before I left home forever.

I've never eaten such *czulent* again. I miss its taste; I miss the feeling on my tongue, on my lips, inside my mouth. I write now and recall, and my mouth begins to water. I feel my lips touch the coarse, hard outer shell of a peeled potato, caramelized under the slow baking process. A slow heat. I bite into this single small peeled potato, brown and aromatic. The hard baked outer skin and soft baked inner texture warm my mouth. I close my eyes, trying to recall the face of my mother.

Photo credit: Monte Nagler

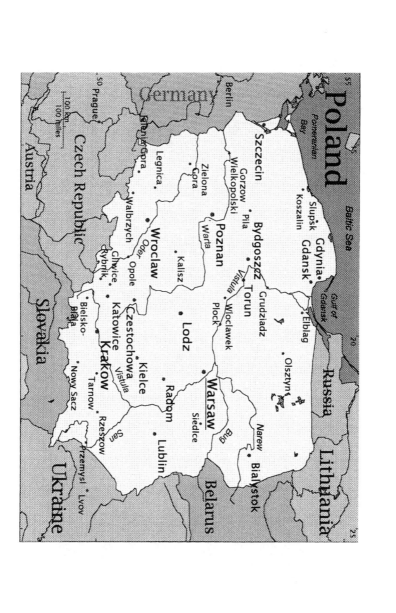

Sobota 19-X-1946 r.

1 Dzisiaj mama kupiłyśmy z całą szkołą w kościele
mi się Skrzyczenie, chodż lekcji dziś nie było.
[Chrzestem... tie w niedzielę też do komunji się
ale mi z tego nie z czego wynikła awantura
z ciotunia musiałam więc zrezygnować.

Środa 18.XII.1946 r.

Wczoraj mieliśmy wizytację w szkole.
U nas byli na historii i polskim
Olbłig meński dość dobre, ja jednak mam
powazny kłopot z powodu mego wzrostu.
Powiedział pan wizytator, że nie mogę
być w VII klasie. W sobotę "mamunia" najdzie do
nami hierowniczki i może coś zołatwie.
Dzisiaj "mamunia" pojechała z "tatunkiem" do
[Wadała], może jutro przyjadzie.

Sobota 21.XII.46r. =

"Mamusia" przyjechała przedwczoraj.
Dzisiaj jest ostatni dzień przed świętami.
Musiała już nie byłam w szkole, bo musiałam
być w sklepie. Wmawiałam panu Szymburskiemu
namiętności, dawałam różne chwyt, nie go oddał
lecz nie było mnie w szkole.

Niedziela 16.XII. 1946 r.

Już dawno nie pisałam do teh mi
jakoś schodziło wciąż nie miałam czasu.
Ponieważ nie śpię już na "górze" nie miałam
z początku gdzie pomieścić swych rzeczy,
hostał więc pomieszanih w szafie na "górze" i dla-
tego tak długo nie pisałam.
Postanowiłam teraz nie chodzić do kina i skła-
dać pieniądze na rower. Nie wiem czy złożę?

Bardzo już dawno nie pisałem, nie miałem...

W ostatnich czasach stał się wprost okropny.
Nie wspominam już o tym, że rzucił się na mnie z nożem
wpadłszy, całkiem zresztą niesłusznie w szał,
lecz te ciągłe sceny w sklepie przy gościach,
to wyzywanie od najgorszych [illegible], to bicie
po plecach i głowie ze wszystkich sił, to są rzeczy,
o których nie prędko się zapomina i które niełatwo
się przebacza. Ale rozpisałam się za wiele o żalach
a tu tymczasem trzeba pisać o wszystkim. Tyle mam rzeczy
do pisania że nie wiem od czego zacząć. A więc przede wszystkim
jest już po wakacjach, które jak już wspominałam były dla mnie
bardzo smutne. Chodzę już od dwuch dni do szkoły i bardzo
jestem zadowolona bo w szkole to jakby nie było zawsze jest
weselej niż w tym sklepie. Wprawdzie i teraz muszę po
przyjściu do szkoły siedzieć w sklepie, ale przynajmniej kilka
godzin jestem w szkole.

Send me ___copies of *Trains* at $14.95 each, plus $3 shipping per book. (Michigan residents please include $.90 state sales tax.)

Name_____

Address_____

City/State/Zip_____

Make your check payable and return to:
Kelton Press, P.O. Box 4236, Jackson, MI 49204

Send me ___copies of *Trains* at $14.95 each, plus $3 shipping per book. (Michigan residents please include $.90 state sales tax.)

Name_____

Address_____

City/State/Zip_____

Make your check payable and return to:
Kelton Press, P.O. Box 4236, Jackson, MI 49204